THE FRONTIERS OF CHINA

THE FRONTIERS
OF CHINA

By

FRANCIS WATSON

FREDERICK A. PRAEGER, *Publishers*

New York • Washington

BOOKS THAT MATTER

Published in the United States of America in 1966
by Frederick A. Praeger, Inc., Publishers
111 Fourth Avenue, New York, N.Y. 10003

© 1966 by Francis Watson
Library of Congress Catalog Card Number: 66-12989
Printed in the United States of America

CONTENTS

CONTENTS

CONTENTS

MAPS

I

COMMUNISM OR
IMPERIALISM?

THE SHAPE OF CHINA

CHINA's long land-frontiers (including by her action in 1950 the southern frontier of Tibet) run with twelve independent or protected States: the USSR, the Mongolian PR, Korea (North), Vietnam (North), Laos, Burma, India, Bhutan, Sikkim, Nepal, Pakistan (*de facto*, west of the Kashmir cease-fire line), and Afghanistan. Britain in Hong Kong, and Portugal in Macao, retain coastal colonies established by treaty; and in Taiwan (Formosa) and the neighbouring offshore islands the rival Chinese Nationalist régime enjoys United Nations status and United States protection.

The Government of the Chinese People's Republic, on taking power in 1949, declared that it would re-examine treaties concluded by its predecessors with foreign powers, and either 'recognize, abrogate, revise or renegotiate them'. This was not in itself a repudiation of inherited international commitments, but a notice of the intention to question their validity as and when the occasion should be judged appropriate in Peking. Between 1960 and 1963 new frontier-agreements were concluded by China with Burma, Nepal, Mongolia, Pakistan and Afghanistan.

In the general configuration of its territory, China to-day can be described in the phrase used by its Communist Government of particular issues with its neighbours. It is 'a problem left over by imperialism'. In plainer language,

9

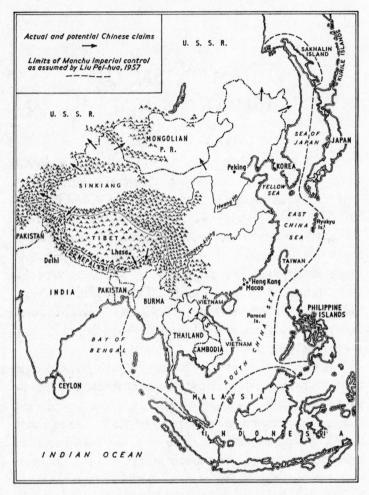

1. China and her Neighbours.

the extent of Peking's control results in very large measure from the interaction of three historic empires in Asia. Two of these, the Chinese and the Russian, have been strengthened as political units by the force of Communist revolution. The third, the British, has been peace-

fully dissolved, leaving to new national States the responsibility of frontier-relations with the power-system to the
North. The subsequent disappearance of French colonial
power from South-East Asia produced a similar confrontation, though under different circumstances. The Japanese Empire, destroyed in World War II, has ceased to
furnish a frontier-question on the Asian mainland. China's
historical relations with the United States, now designated
the 'leader of the imperialist camp' in Communist propaganda, did not involve strictly territorial considerations.

Any discussion of a frontier-question must proceed
from some basic attitude to territorial possession and
national sovereignty. The simplification of the idea of
Communist-Imperialist struggle propounded—even in
disagreement—by Peking and Moscow, has allowed it to
be assumed that the liquidation of empires is an orthodox
Communist principle, together with the right of subject
peoples to establish their own inviolable frontiers. It is the
persistence of this theme that has given a startling air to
the exposure of the great-power element in Communist
political behaviour. For a Communist State to suppress
national minorities within its own territories, and to make
claims or attacks upon the territory of others, appeared as
a contradiction or as a failure to practice an ideal. Reaction
to such a spectacle has consequently tended to vary between revulsion and incredulity.

The self-assertive politics of the major Communist
States are not, however, incompatible with Marxist ideas.
The original Marxist preoccupation was with the large
and powerful State as the essential foundation of Communism, and it has persisted. On questions of national
self-determination and sovereignty the doctrine was at
first negative. It was the tactics of revolution within the

multi-national Russian Empire which demanded a new point in the Communist programme, 'because and only because', as Lenin explained to his followers, nationalist movements had become importantly active inside the Russian, Persian, Turkish and Chinese Empires. The eventual consolidation of Soviet power within the frontiers of the Tsarist dominions required first the encouragement, and subsequently the defeat, of nationalist and federalist aspirations. Theoretical cover for the operation was supplied by Stalin, in the gloss that 'the right of nations to self-determination' must be subordinated to 'the right of the working-class' (i.e. of the Soviet State) 'to consolidate its power'.

The large centralized State as 'the only path to Socialism' was equally accepted by Mao Tse-tung and the Chinese Communists. So was the tactical requirement of a declaration in favour of self-determination for non-Chinese peoples within the inherited imperial frontiers. This appeared in the constitution drafted by the Chinese Communist Party in 1931, eighteen years before it achieved power. It was there undertaken that the minority peoples 'may either join the Union of Chinese Soviets or secede from it and form their own State as they may prefer'. In the event the Chinese People's Republic became a unitary State incorporating 'minority autonomous areas', thereby abandoning even the nominal federal principle, with its dead-letter of permissive secession, of the Russian Soviet constitution.

A more important difference is to be found in the relative poverty of the imperial inheritance to which Sun Yat-sen and his Republicans succeeded in 1912,* and

* Yuan Shih-kai secured the Presidency with the compliance of Sun Yat-sen, whose party was later renamed the Kuomintang or Nationalist Party.

Mao Tse-tung and his Communists in 1949. In the Soviet Union irredentism—as distinct from the general ambition of extending Communism—was in no great evidence before the Second World War. But the territories and advantages then acquired by the USSR represented the fulfilment of historic though outwardly abandoned imperial ambitions of frontier-extension.* In the case of China irredentism was an essential feature of the political climate in which the Chinese Communist Party was established and operated. As a target for internal dissatisfaction the imperial régime had already been removed. The tendency to externalize grievances was therefore strengthened, with prompt assistance from Japan in her Twenty-One Demands of 1915. To respond to a national dynamic was for the Chinese not a question of consolidating an extensive dominion but of restoring one that had been despoiled. But since the chief of its despoilers, in the territorial sense, had been the rival Russian Empire, a powerful effect was caused by the Soviet announcement of July 1919 that 'The Government of the Workers and Peasants has . . . declared null and void . . . the treaties which were to enable the Russian Government of the Tsar and his allies to enslave the people of the East and principally the people of China.' This declaration (subsequently known as the Karakhan Declaration) undoubtedly played a part in the conversion of Mao Tse-tung to Marxism, a conversion which by March 1920 (according to his own testimony) had taken place 'in theory and to some extent in action'. The Chinese Communist Party was founded in the following year, and for

---

* Soviet frontiers in Europe were extended to take in nearly 180,000 sq. miles of neighbouring territory containing more than 21 million people, while in the Far East the 'former rights' of Tsarist Russia were invoked against the defeated Japanese.

its first eleven years retained the closest links with Moscow.

CONSEQUENCES OF COMMUNISM

Soviet failure to implement the Karakhan Declaration, however much it rankled, could only confirm the Marxist belief in power-politics. In adapting the great-power foundation of Communism to their national aspirations, both Russians and Chinese had the support of traditional attitudes—a Messianic tradition in Russia, the pride of 'Middle Kingdom' civilization in China. But the Chinese, with a special sense of national grievance, have shown fewer inhibitions in asserting territorial ownership. Expressions parallel with 'China's Sinkiang' or 'China's Tibet' have not been used by the USSR in relation to, say, Kazakhstan: still less to Outer Mongolia, now the People's Republic, which would undoubtedly have been 'China's Mongolia' if the Chinese Communists had been in a position to implement a claim upon the territory stronger in several ways than that which they enforced upon Tibet. Nor has the Chinese Communist Party found it necessary to justify Chinese Imperial expansion as 'a progressive factor', as Soviet ideologists have argued in the case of the Tsarist conquests.

It has often been said that the replacement of China's political chaos by any strong central government would be followed by a revival of frontier-questions. The Chinese People's Government, indeed, found it necessary to answer, in its memorandum to the Indian Government on 26 December 1959, the 'rather prevalent observation that China has now grown strong and, like certain Chinese rulers in history or modern imperialists, would seek expansion abroad'. The fact that it was the Chinese Communist Party that captured power in 1949 was to have particular consequences in frontier-relations, as well as the general result of modernizing the Chinese consciousness of imperial mission. To distinguish some of these effects:

(i) The ideological impetus of Communism stimulated and transformed the operations for control of the non-Han peoples in outlying areas and the development of their territories which any strongly-established régime would have attempted. This brought Chinese armies and Chinese settlers into regions which had scarcely seen them in the past, and dictated the course of new communications. One of the avowed objects of the Chinese move into Tibet in 1950 was 'to defend China's frontiers'–i.e. to militarize them.

(ii) Relations with Soviet Russia, affecting the larger part of China's land-frontiers, were established in ideological terms which appeared to suppress the powerful factor of national rivalry. The problems arising between 'fraternal Socialist States', and the methods of solving them, were distinguished from those that might arise between China and her non-Communist neighbours. The eventual widening of the Sino-Soviet schism towards the revival of frontier-disputes therefore found each party accusing the other of being the first to introduce 'problems between States' into the debate.

(iii) Ideology also produced the serviceable dogma that a 'Socialist State' cannot *by definition* commit aggression. Frequently asserted in Chinese Communist propaganda, this was sometimes adumbrated even in official communications (e.g. in the note to India of 26 December 1959). Echoed at the same time by spokesmen of the Communist Party of India, it inevitably worsened the frontier-dispute between the two countries. Titoist rejections of the proposition were attacked by Peking as 'revisionist' heresy.

(iv) Conditions of internal Communist control of opinion facilitated manipulation in the Chinese conduct of frontier-diplomacy with non-Communist neighbours. In the dispute with India, for example, officially organized demonstrations and statements in China were invested with the authority of public opinion, while free comment in India—by individuals, in parliament, or in the press—was used for official Peking charges against the Indian Government.

(v) To the uncertain political potential of Overseas Chinese communities in South-East Asia the emergence of a Communist China added a further problem of loyalties. Communist Parties inside the new national democracies on China's borders, accepting the requisite of an 'established base' for revolutionary activity, paid particular attention to frontier-zones. The strength of the external political attachment can be seen in the case of the Communist Party of India, where even after Chinese invasion the pro-Chinese faction was persistent enough to cause a split in the Party.

For any country sharing a boundary with China, the extent to which the Communist régime is prepared to revive the territorial claims of past empires is clearly of the first importance. The Communist system in itself offers no restraint to such ambitions. It postulates the expanded State as the area of development, and it seeks to obliterate ethnic, linguistic, religious and cultural factors as the bases of independent nationalism. The only restraint on Chinese policy in this matter arises from realistic appreciations of the need for a peaceful period of development within existing frontiers, and of the anticipated resistance to attempts to change them at any one time or place.

TRADITIONAL ATTITUDES

Even to define 'China' raises certain difficulties. These have commonly been met by historians by reference to a Chinese civilization rather than to a Chinese nation— a theme which can readily be preserved in a modern framework of ideological supremacy transcending national distinctions. In the history of frontiers it has meant the acceptance of a Chinese territorial entity composed of what was once called 'China Proper' together with 'Chinese Dependencies'. At the end of the 19th century 'China Proper' was still, roughly speaking, the 'Middle Kingdom' of the last purely Chinese dynasty of the Ming

Emperors, lying south of the Great Wall and east of Tibet. But the only frontier-zones of today's 'People's China' corresponding to those of the old 'Chinese China' are those with the Shan States of Burma, Vietnam and Laos. Even the vast Manchu (Ch'ing) conquests did not extend the administrative boundaries of 'China Proper' until the last years of the Empire, when Manchuria began to be incorporated and Sinkiang became a nominal province. The Republican Government of the Kuomintang carried the process of incorporation further. But the novelty of the Communist unitary Chinese State is to be seen in its preoccupation, after several millennia of imperial history, with the problem of 'minority peoples' and their resistance to 'Great Han chauvinism'.

The simplest fact of Chinese frontier-attitudes in ancient tradition is illustrated by the location of the Great Wall. The long sea-frontier presented no danger until comparatively recent times, nor was the danger understood when it appeared. South of China's intensively cultivated alluvial plains the mountain-regions were not impassable, but the lie of range and river favoured infiltration towards the south rather than invasion from it. On the west the Chinese homelands were buttressed by more formidable ranges separating them from India and Tibet, north of which ran the long and difficult desert-route of western communication—a route which, though it might lend itself to raiding as well as trading, did not invite occupation. The danger was from the north, and in filling the gap the Great Wall also completed the definition of monsoon-China, thickly settled and cultivated and culturally advanced, as distinct from the outer wilderness of desert and grassland and plateau ranged by nomadic, primitive and periodically dangerous tribes.

The Wall, however, was neither a guarantee nor even a symbol of a defined frontier. In the 4th century A.D., and again in the 12th, China was invaded and partially conquered from the north, and in the 13th century it was entirely overrun by the Mongols and annexed to their enormous empire. Nor, on the other hand, were the natural and artificial boundaries of settled territory ever regarded by the rulers of China as limiting their own authority. Agricultural settlement was pushed north of the Wall into Inner Mongolia. Expeditionary armies from time to time enforced varying degrees of subservience to the Imperial Court at immense distances, and the ceremonial of tribute was preserved even where the realities of power had changed or vanished—or where they had never existed, as in the devices of the later Manchu Court to treat Western deputations as tributaries.

Even after the abdication of the Manchus and the revolution of 1911, therefore, there was at least a psychological background in which China's frontiers were not viewed by the Chinese as having been fixed either by geography or by history, and certainly not by the history of a weak period of Chinese central government. Prof. C. P. Fitzgerald has written:

China was the civilized world; for centuries this was perfectly true as far as Chinese experience reached, and the idea remained firm in Chinese minds long after it had ceased to be true in fact. Territory once won for civilization must not be given back to barbarism; therefore, territory which was once Chinese must forever remain so, and if lost, must be recovered at the first opportunity. Such loss cannot be legal or valid; it is at best a recognition of passing weakness. The whole growth of the Chinese Empire, throughout more than 3,000 years, had been built on this principle; the barbarians were conquered, then absorbed and turned into Chinese by slow assimilation and cultural influence. To deny this process, to claim that it had, or should, come to an end, was to Chinese thought a denial of the right, a recognition of failure.*

ASPECTS OF FRONTIER-POLICY

In so far as this way of thinking persists (and there is much to suggest that it does so to at least some degree), it has an effective corollary. The basic claim being almost mystically extensive, there is a tendency to avoid definition; and it is fair to conclude that this has served conscious purposes in the policies of the Chinese People's Government. With the prospect of a vague but general intention to call her existing frontiers in question, China has been able to hold all her neighbours under some degree of suspended sentence. How serious the threat may be has depended upon a current view of China's ability to enforce it. But even this is provided for by the phrase 'at the appropriate time' in Chinese communications, used against a background of propaganda looking confidently into an extended future—as of an empire in time as well as space. Nor is this picture destroyed by the evidence of frontier-agreements entered upon by the Chinese People's Government, or by the manner of their negotiation.

The timing of the Chinese approach to a settlement has varied greatly in response to political requirements, from the unhurried treatment of the first initiatives of Burma and Pakistan to the sudden agreement with the Mongolian People's Republic. The calculations of opportunism are readily made, but in the absence of recognized pressures there is evidently much to be said, in the Peking view, for an indefinitely open question. An imprecise but basic dissatisfaction with an existing frontier having been

* In *The World Today*, January 1963 (Royal Institute of International Affairs).

made known, even the prospect of negotiation can be put forward under a colour of concession, with a future settlement as a mark of Chinese beneficence rather than as the ratification of authentic territorial rights. So long as the question is kept open there is also the possibility of linking Chinese 'concessions' with expectations of appropriate political behaviour by the neighbour-country.

Thus Chou En-lai's 1956 offer to recognize China's McMahon Line boundaries with India and Burma was made to the Prime Ministers of both countries (after complaints from both about current Chinese maps) on account of 'the friendly relations subsisting between both countries and China'. It was honoured in the case of Burma, but repudiated in the case of India, the Chinese Government having in the meantime taken offence at Indian reactions to the Tibetan revolt and its suppression. In the later case of Mongolia, although very little documentation of the Chinese frontier-agreement was released, there were good reasons for concluding that Peking had expected in return (vainly, as it turned out) at least a show of Mongolian neutrality in the Sino-Soviet dispute.

The disposition to trade a border-alignment for a political advantage illustrates Peking's apparently basic view of frontier-questions as political and ideological rather than juridical. The more direct bargaining of territory for territory is also accepted as a negotiating technique; but its use has necessarily been complicated by Chinese regard for the tradition quoted above—that 'territory which was once Chinese must forever remain so'. Exchanges which had an important bearing on a settlement with Burma were postponed by Chou En-lai's invocation of this principle. In the dispute with India there were early (though extremely discreet) indications that the Chinese might be prepared to pay for the vital Ladakh salient with a transfer of territory in another border-zone. But the most reasonable *quid pro quo*, the contrary Tibetan salient of the Chumbi Valley (which breaks the watershed-line in a deep and awkward indentation between Sikkim and Bhutan) could not be put on offer without damage to possessive Chinese doctrine.* What *was* put on offer, in a series of manœuvres which the Indians can be excused for regarding as first tortuous and finally blatant, was the 32,000 square miles of territory south of the McMahon Line which formed the Indian North-East Frontier Agency. For whatever arguments the Chinese might find for questioning India's title to this area, they themselves had no title to anything but minor border-adjustments— and indeed had sought no more than these in setting up their own markers, some forty years earlier, at selected points a few miles below the McMahon alignment. The entire Chinese use of this large area as a factor in the dispute depended upon a cartographical device intended by its Kuomintang originators to disprove Tibet's capacity to treat with other nations. And in all these circumstances Chou En-lai's offer to recognize the McMahon Line as a boundary might have been thought hardly less sinister than its subsequent withdrawal.

'Cartographical aggression' has been the name given in neighbouring countries to the publication of apparently menacing Chinese maps which, on representations being made to Peking, were broadly disavowed but neither

---

* This does not rule out the possibility that an Indian request for the Chumbi Valley, against a settlement of Chinese requirements in Ladakh, might have been taken up if it had been made at a propitious stage. But the difficulties of recognizing and seizing such an opportunity were considerable. The idea was in fact floated in Delhi, but defeated inside the Government – apparently by the mistrust and resentment which Peking's conduct of the dispute had by then aroused. See below, p. 113.

corrected nor withdrawn. Whatever the political intentions of this practice, its political effects could have been
readily foreseen. But it has not been the only indication of
a special Chinese attitude to what, at some stage of any
frontier-question, must come to be seen as 'the facts of
the situation'. These were what Nehru regarded as deter-
minable by a joint examination of the maps, treaties,
evidence of administration and other documents on which
each side relied for its case. The reluctance with which
Chou En-lai assented to this proposal was made perfectly
clear. So was his preference for a prior agreement on a
number of 'points of principle'. Since some of these important 'points'—for example the postulate that the entire
length of the frontier was open to fresh consideration—
were not likely to stand up against any factual scrutiny, it
may be said that the Indian insistence on this procedure en-
sured an eventual Chinese substitute of force for argument.

In the matter of treaty-evidence the Tibetan frontier
(forming by far the greater part of the Sino-Indian contact) was that to which the Chinese hope of invalidating all
previous agreements was most tenaciously applied. To
discuss treaties in any historical sense must endanger their
assumption of legal sovereignty over Tibet. To discuss
them officially, in sessions that might eventually be publicly reported, would expose them in a tangle of contradic-
tions even at strong points of their case. A general distaste
for the treaties of the past, as the documentation of periods
of relative weakness in China's history, may have had some
effect on the Chinese attitude to maps—even, in some cases,
to Chinese maps, which they disavowed as having been
produced under foreign pressure or influence. But this is
not enough to account for the indifference or objection to
topographical detail shown—at all events initially—by the

Communist rulers of a nation which had once held map-makers and historians in great respect. The official exchanges between Delhi and Peking on frontier-incidents were notable from the outset for the Indian practice of furnishing co-ordinates of longitude and latitude; but it was only later, and with difficulty, that the Chinese were brought to introduce detailed data into their reports and allegations. Even when the joint examination of the question by officials of both sides was about to begin, the Chinese had no map available for the purpose on a scale greater than 1 : 5 million. The Indians, who wanted to work with maps of 1 : 1 million,* at length agreed to admit the Chinese maps in order to get the talks moving. At their sixth meeting, the Chinese introduced a new map, in which their claims in Ladakh had been advanced by some 2,000 square miles beyond the 12,000 square miles originally objected to by India. And what seems significant is that when China's Foreign Minister, Chen Yi, took up the matter in a speech of 6 December 1961, it was not to justify the discrepancy but rather to ignore it. A 'clear and definite' description of the boundary, he then maintained, was given in *both* the Chinese maps.

The Chinese attitude to natural features as a principle of frontier-settlement has been somewhat confusing. Although Chou En-lai admitted them to consideration in the 'points' which he urged upon the Indian Government, they were later rejected in a general sense, possibly because of the river-line followed by the 'unequal' frontier-settlements with Russia in the North-East. And although the Chinese have in some cases (Burma and Pakistan) appeared to accept a watershed-line in mountainous areas,

* The scale stated by the U.N. Cartographical Organization to be the least permitting reasonably detailed study.

23

there is a good deal to suggest a historic Chinese preference for 'overlooking' a neighbour by a frontier carried
down the further slopes of a dividing range.

AN 1840 BASELINE?

'How far back are we to go?' asked Nehru despairingly at
a particularly infructuous stage in the Chinese exploration
of the shifting power-limits of the remote past. Chinese
irredentism has given no final indications of its horizon,
and Sino-Soviet polemics have even revived—though
perhaps hardly seriously—historical issues of the Mongol
conquests of the 13th and 14th centuries. The territorial
grievances on which Peking has become most specific,
however, belong to the 19th century, in the latter era of
the Manchu (Ch'ing) Empire, itself the result of invasion
of China from the North.

The initial declaration of principle (29 September
1949) as to the reconsideration by the CPR Government
of previous treaties and agreements, had been phrased to
refer to those 'concluded between the Kuomintang and
foreign Governments'. This position having been taken
up, the Sino-Soviet (Chiang-Stalin) treaty and agreements
of 1945 were superseded and declared null and void by
the thirty-year Treaty of Friendship, Alliance and Mutual
Assistance concluded between Moscow and Peking on
14 February 1950. But in securing this alliance, Mao Tse-
tung had to confirm—at all events overtly—the relinquish-
ment of China's tenacious claim to Outer Mongolia which
Stalin had extracted from Chiang Kai-shek in the name of
Mongolian 'independence'. Other territorial questions
were either suppressed or tacitly postponed, and nothing
more was heard for thirteen years of the basic Chinese
stand on treaty-revision.

On 8 March 1963, however, the 1949 declaration was recalled in an important *People's Daily* editorial, reacting to some taunts of Khrushchev on the failure of the Chinese Communists to 'liberate' Taiwan, Hong Kong and Macao. The word 'Kuomintang' in the original declaration was replaced in this article by the phrase 'previous Chinese Governments', thus including among challengeable agreements the 'unequal treaties' accepted by a weakened Chinese Empire in the second half of the 19th century. Twelve countries were alleged to have 'carried out unbridled aggression against China' in that period. Many of these 'aggressions' were non-territorial in character, and had in fact long since been voluntarily renounced. Of the territorial beneficiaries, of course, the Russians had been the largest: and (despite rhetorical repentance) the most retentive. They were indicted in the *People's Daily* article in respect of four 19th-century treaties: those of Aigun (1858), Tientsin (1858), Peking (1860) and Ili (or St Petersburg, 1881).

The time-scale of this exposure of grievances fits in with the first of the three periods into which Chinese Communist historians of the present day customarily divide their revolutionary era. This first period, opening in 1840 with the mis-called 'Opium Wars' and ending with the May Fourth Movement of 1919, is named 'The Old Democratic Revolutionary Era'. The second period, 'The New Democratic Revolutionary Era', extends from 1919 to the establishment of the People's Republic in 1949; and the third, not yet concluded, is 'The Era of Socialist Construction'.

Thus the 'China' of the Communist scale of measurement is that of 1840, when the frontiers of the Manchu Empire were still at their greatest extent. Although this need not mean that the leaders of Communist China are irrevocably committed to restoring the boundaries of 1840, it does mean that frontier-questions are liable to be considered with a map of China as at that period within mental reach, even if it is not produced in evidence. At least one case is now widely known of the publication of such a map for students in today's People's Republic, designed to show 'the Chinese territories taken by the Imperialists in the Old Democratic Revolutionary Era (1840–1919)'. The book which carried this map on its facing-page was Liu Pei-hua's *Brief History of Modern China*, published in Peking in 1952 and reissued two years later in a second edition. Reproduction of this map and its accompanying documentation outside China at the end of 1962* produced reactions which Peking had eventually to counter by denying official responsibility. In the USSR, as a Communist State, this disclaimer must have been particularly unconvincing; and on 2 September 1964, *Pravda* joined the list of foreign publications that had drawn conclusions from the map.

What can hardly be disputed is that for ten years Chinese students had been permitted, if not encouraged, to believe that 'Chinese territories taken by the Imperialists in the Old Democratic Revolutionary Era' stood to be recovered by means of the liquidation of imperialism in the 'Era of Socialist Construction'. A similar implication, though without the ideology, had appeared in a number of maps circulating under the previous Kuomintang régime.

---

* An Indian student in Peking, Mr Ghanshyam Mehta, obtained a copy of the book in 1960 after talking to Nepalese fellow-students who had drawn the attention of their Prime Minister to it during his official visit. After returning to India Mr Mehta gave no publicity to the matter until the Chinese military attack of November 1962 and the accompanying Peking propaganda attributing to Nehru the intention of creating an expanded Indian Empire.

26

COMMUNISM OR IMPERIALISM?

In these, Prof. Fitzgerald has observed, 'the word for "lost to" is the word which in Chinese official histories is used to record the loss of a town or city by the emperor to rebels: it literally means "betrayed" '. In the case of the Communist textbook, the processes by which the territories of the Manchu Empire had been reduced were clearly suggested as arbitrary and invalid. China's 'Great North-West', for example, shown in the map to cover large areas of the Russian SFSR and the Kazakh and Kirghiz Soviet Republics, 'was seized by Imperialist Russia under the Treaty of Chuguchak, 1864'.

FRONTIERS AND SEMI-FRONTIERS

The import of the Liu Pei-hua map (or of the ideas which allowed it to be published) is more than a matter of nostalgia for lost conquests. What is significant is that the boundaries here assigned to the China of 1840 go in many cases far beyond the limits of Manchu or any previous imperial rule. They encompass foreign lands and peoples which the Empire neither controlled nor administered, where the most that could be claimed was a tradition of tributary relationship. We are thus confronted with the persistence into modern times, and under a Communist system of government, of an archaic theory of vassalage which virtually overlooks frontiers and minimizes their effective meaning.

Neither Mongolia nor Tibet, in this map, have any frontiers with China. They are namelessly absorbed. Highly disputable claims to Chinese sovereignty (in the Mongolian instance signed away by the Chinese People's Government itself four years before the book was published) are here converted into an extinguishing possession. A southern frontier for China is indicated, taking in

the claim-line subsequently advanced against India. But
this is only a semi-frontier. Beyond it a line purporting to
represent the Chinese borders of 1840 appropriates
Nepal, Sikkim and Bhutan, the Indian State of Assam*
and a part of East Pakistan, the Andaman Islands, the
whole of Burma, Thailand, Malaya and Singapore, and
the States of the former French Indo-China. Winding
through the Pacific the line encloses (besides Taiwan) the
southern Sulu archipelago of the Philippines, the Ryukyu
Islands to the south of Japan and Sakhalin to the north of
it. Korea is also retained, and so is the Chinese claim to
the Soviet maritime territories and the 'Great North-East'
beyond the Amur River.

It is not necessary to examine in detail the fluctuating
history of the influence of Chinese dynasties beyond their
southern borders, nor the grounds—self-chosen and often
shadowy—on which they held the listed countries to be
vassal States. The point is that any degree of formal vassalage, or none, appears here as a title to inclusion within
the Chinese boundaries. In many instances the 'losses'
said to have been sustained by China after 1840 made
little difference to the ceremonial exchanges fixed at
traditional intervals. In some, for example in Nepal,
certain observances could be taken to signify that China
was the tributary, rather than the other way round. But on
the evidence of this map the Chinese make no distinction
between 'losses' resulting from the advance of other imperial powers and those entailed in an act of independence.

Thus Annam (the name given to the combined States
of Indo-China) is described in 1952 as 'captured by the
French in 1885' (from the Chinese); Burma 'became a

* The Indian North-East Frontier Agency is not shown as having ever been
'lost' by China.

part of the British Empire in 1886' (after Assam had been 'given to Britain by Burma in 1826')*; and Thailand or Siam, whose frontiers and neutrality were jointly guaranteed by Britain and France, earns the complaint that it was 'declared "independent" under joint Anglo-French control in 1904'. Nepal likewise 'went under the British after "independence" in 1898'.

The preservation by a Communist régime of antique concepts of vassalage might seem well adapted to the pattern of satellite States grouped about a modern Power. But today the Chinese view of a tributary does not necessarily, or immediately, require its adoption of the Communist system. Indeed, where a 'lost' vassal has come under Communist rule (North Vietnam, North Korea), Peking has had a harder struggle for control because of the existence of a rival protector in Moscow. What is underlined, however, by the sequence we are considering is that the question of frontiers is for the Chinese predominantly a political rather than a legalistic matter. What is a frontier as seen from one side, the neighbour's side, may be a semi-frontier from the other, where what matters is a horizon of influence.

The Chinese view of history since 1840, no less than the present Chinese ideology, insists that this horizon is not to be gained without the preliminary exclusion of any other influence. Peking's support for the neutrality of the border-State of Laos, as internationally proposed, was clearly not a vote for the independence of the Laotian Kingdom but for the removal of any external obstacle to

---

* After repelling the great Chinese invasion of 1769, undertaken at the height of Manchu imperial power, the Burmese armies of Alaungpaya's dynasty had ravaged Arakan, Manipur and parts of Assam. The challenge to British power in Bengal led to the First Anglo-Burmese War (1824–6) after which Burma ceded Arakan and renounced any claim upon Assam and Manipur.

the hegemony of its one powerful neighbour: a hegemony to be exercised as effectively across a frontier as in violation of it. The Treaties of Friendship and Mutual Non-Aggression offered to Burma and to Nepal as logical sequences of frontier-settlement may be said to represent the nearest thing to an exclusive relationship which 'neutralist' nation-states can be brought to consider. Burma accepted the relationship. Nepal modified it by declining the Non-Aggression Pact. With India, a much larger State with an influential international position, the frontier-question took a very different course. There was small likelihood that India, however friendly as a matter of broad policy, would accept any hint of exclusiveness in her relations with China. Yet this is what the People's Government at length demanded, in the Chinese Ambassador's 'appeal' of May, 1959, for a realignment of Indian foreign policy in harmony with the Chinese Communist view.

The Indian rejection of this approach was inevitable. Negotiations conducted upon such a condition, even if they should prove territorially satisfactory, would produce a semi-frontier, not a settlement. Equally inevitable was the result of the Indian rejection, which demonstrably hardened the Chinese attitude to the frontier-question itself.

II

THE NORTHERN MARCHES
IN HISTORY

EMPIRES IN CONTACT

THE boundaries between the Chinese People's Republic and the Union of Soviet Socialist Republics extend—even when the Mongolian section has been excluded as defining a separate State—for approximately 4,500 miles. They form the world's longest frontier between two States. In its origins, however, this is not a national frontier, even if it be considered to be in the course of becoming so by the forced integration of minority peoples. The Sino-Soviet boundaries are the result of the shrinkage, over a period of at least three centuries, of the zones of contact between two expanding land-empires.

Neither the Chinese Revolution in 1911 nor the Russian Revolution in 1917, brought this process to finality. But after the elimination of a third party—the Japanese Empire—in the Second World War, the new relationship between Communist régimes in Moscow and Peking appeared to point towards frontier-stabilization. Not only were the two Powers linked for the first time in a bilateral alliance. Both put forward a dogma of 'special relations between Socialist States' from which the rivalries and conflicts of the capitalist world were to be eliminated. The long advance of each side in search of its own 'final frontier' was implied to belong to the discredited past.

During the latter part of that period of advance, however, Russian power had played the major expansionist rôle, Chinese power that of the weakened victim. This fact had received Russian acknowledgment, after the overthrow of the Tsars, in the Declaration addressed on 25 July 1919 'to the Chinese nation and the Governments of Northern and Southern China'.

> The Government of the Russian Soviet Federated Socialist Republic declares as void all the treaties concluded by the former Government of Russia with China, renounces all the annexations of Chinese territory, all the concessions in China, and returns to China free of charge, and for ever, all that was ravenously taken from her by the Tsar's Government and by the Russian bourgeoisie.

Resounding rather than specific, the Karakhan Declaration was, as we know, never implemented. The most that it produced in respect of frontiers was the 1924 agreement by the Soviet and Chinese (KMT) Governments to 'redemarcate their national boundaries' at a Conference which, so far as there is any evidence, never succeeded in meeting. The agreement was contained in the Sino-Soviet Treaty and Declaration of 31 May 1924, with the further statement that 'pending such redemarcation' the existing boundaries would be maintained.

The Karakhan Declaration has not, on the other hand, been disavowed, and in the 1924 Treaty it was evidently supposed, with similar statements that had followed it, to be guiding Soviet policy. It may therefore seem strange that the Chinese Communists, when reviving territorial questions in the *People's Daily* article of March 1963, made no appeal to it, preferring to cite 'unequal treaties' which they had long ago broadly pronounced to be null and void.

It may be that the Chinese will yet produce these early renunciations in proof of the present Soviet Government's bad faith and departure from revolutionary ideals. But it seems equally possible that they have no wish to let the open argument turn upon principles of self-determination which might be invoked to their own disadvantage. These are what the Russian Communists have already successfully exploited in the case of Mongolia. And the Karakhan Declaration had contained a precautionary clause to the same effect:

> The Soviet Government has renounced the conquests made by the Tsarist Government which deprived China of Manchuria and other areas. Let the people living in those areas themselves decide within the frontiers of which State they wish to dwell, and what form of government they wish to establish in their own countries.

In the case of Manchuria the Soviet Government may have felt that these rhetorical sentiments were sufficiently satisfied by concluding with the Manchurian warlord, Chang Tso-lin, an agreement supplementary to the Sino-Soviet Treaty of 1924. It was the author of the Declarations, Leo Karakhan, who finalized these arrangements, and it was he who candidly commented upon them: 'At present the Soviet Union is gaining a firm foothold in the Far East by occupying one of the most important positions of which its enemies were trying to deprive it.' In 1929 this position was defended by force in an undeclared frontier-war with the Chinese Nationalists. By 1932 it had been surrendered, not to China but to Japan. In the remainder of the vast zone of Sino-Russian contact, any degree of autonomy for its peoples had for more than a century depended upon the distance at which effective Chinese or Russian power could be kept by other factors, or the success with which the one might be played off against the other. As to the decision 'within the frontiers of which State they wish to dwell' the Kirghiz and Kazakh peoples could vote only with their feet. Many of them did so, in a fluctuating and increasingly desperate response to the dictation of events.

It will be clear that an important factor in frontier-history has been the extent of active colonization from either side in the areas intervening between the two centres of power. From the Chinese side especially, where the use of colonization in the strategy of politics was relatively slow to develop, this helps to distinguish the three main zones of contact: the Central Asian Area, the Mongolian Area and the Manchurian Area. Though the Manchurian Area has a long history of Chinese settlement it had been a policy of the Manchu Emperors to preserve their original patrimony by discouraging immigration from China Proper. But throughout the 19th century their decrees on this subject proved less and less effective; and in 1878, with Russification proceeding intensively beyond the Amur River, the Peking policy was reversed. Chinese peasant migration from Inner to Outer Mongolia had likewise been stagnant, and began to increase only after the administrative absorption of Manchuria. But attempts to push it forward in a systematic pattern played into the hands of Mongolian nationalism and Russian calculation. In Sinkiang, the 'New Province' of 1884, the first serious Chinese colonization was left to the Government of Mao Tse-tung.

THE CENTRAL ASIAN AREA

In the 15th century Muscovite Russia and Ming China were well over 2,000 miles apart at the nearest points, separated by deserts, mountains and steppelands and by a variety of peoples both settled and nomadic. By the 1880's the moving frontiers of Tsarist and Manchu expansion in Central Asia had met, dividing the intermediate lands and principalities into Russian and Chinese Turkestan.

The Russian continental expansion had been partly military in its motive and defensive in its origins, beginning with the liquidation of the menacing Tartar Khanates and never quite losing the memory of the Mongol invasions of Europe. The name of Chinghiz (Jenghiz) Khan indeed, to judge by its reappearance in Soviet-Chinese polemics, is still one to conjure with. But the Russian advance had also a significantly colonizing character, with imperial policy sometimes leading and sometimes merely following the outward movement of dispossessed peasants, fugitive rebels and persecuted religious dissenters.

The Chinese traditions of penetration and even of power in Central Asia, though long interrupted, were of great antiquity. In the 2nd century B.C. the Han Emperors, engaged in a desperate struggle with the Hsiung Nu—a nomadic Turki people whom they looked upon as scarcely human—sought for tribal alliances in the far West while defending the Great Wall in the North. This process culminated, at the peak of the dynasty's success, in the inclusion of what was later called Sinkiang in the territories of the Empire; and at the end of the 1st century A.D. a Chinese army had not only consolidated control over all the chiefs of the Turkestan oases but had advanced, for the first and only time, to the edge of Europe on the Caspian Sea. With the collapse of the Han Empire the Chinese tide receded, and fourteen centuries were to pass before it flowed strongly again in the Manchu expansion into Turkestan. But there had been in the 7th century a temporary restoration of the connection under the T'ang Emperors, and in the 13th century the engulfing of both China and Central Asia in the almost world-wide Mongol dominion.

The cyclic tradition was thus established. But from the Chinese side there was nothing that really matched the protracted process of Muscovite advance and settlement beyond the Volga. Even under the Manchu Emperors, Sinkiang remained a region of alien exile for disgraced officials and other offenders rather than a field for pioneers. The fact that these exiles and their families, few as they were, were privileged by taxation and otherwise, did nothing to reconcile the peoples among whom they lived to their own political condition. Armed revolts were frequent, bloody and difficult to deal with, since the area of Chinese occupation was less accessible to the central power than were the Russian conquests. The most successful of these risings, that of Yakub Beg in 1864, wrested authority from the Manchus for thirteen years, establishing a separate State which dealt directly with foreign Governments. The Russians sent missions to Yakub Beg and obtained a commercial treaty, and similar enterprises by the British-Indian Government drew serious attention to the feasible—though formidable—southern approaches through Ladakh.

For the Russians the success of Yakub Beg offered particular advantages, exposing the shadowy nature of Peking's authority and at the same time hastening its need for a settlement in the area of contiguity. And one result was to be the establishment of a Russian salient into Sinkiang in the region of Kuldja on the Ili River. This relatively small but important area, midway in the zone of Sino-Russian contact between the Pamir junction and the Mongolian frontier in the Altai, is one of the historic gates of Inner Asia. The Ili, flowing westwards out of

Sinkiang, not only divides the long mountain-ranges in a widening valley but is navigable for trade and fertile in pasturage. Historically it has provided a natural corridor for the movement of nomadic or raiding peoples. In Russian eyes its military significance was considerable and even symbolic, since it was through this gate that Chinghiz Khan's Mongol cavalry had poured westwards. By 1854, ten years before the revolt of Yakub Beg, the Russian expansion had been extended south-east of Lake Balkhash into the open country reaching to the foothills of the Tien Shan; and it was supported by the construction of forts, settlements and communications—forerunners of the Turk-Sib Railway. Even where a nominal Chinese overlordship was acknowledged, the base of Chinese authority was distant by a difficult journey of six to twelve months. Russia was consequently able to secure trade advantages on the upper Ili, and in the Tarbagatai area farther north.

Territorial consolidation was another matter. By the Treaty of Peking in 1860 the Chinese were compelled to accept the completion of the Tsar's Far Eastern Provinces. But the clauses relating to Central Asia marked only the beginning of delimitation, providing for a joint survey of the area of claim and contact from the foothills of the Altai in the north to the Khanate of Kokand under the brow of the Pamir. And for four years the Chinese Commissioners disputed and delayed the painful process. It had been agreed that a boundary should be mapped along the line of hills where the Chinese maintained permanent pickets. But since there were also movable Chinese pickets well to the west in lower country, an argument developed with the Russian Commissioners not unlike that precipitated with India, more than a century later, by the Chinese interpretation of 'actual control'.

The critical defection in Sinkiang put an end to these tactics. The year of Yakub Beg was also the year of the Treaty of Chuguchak (or of Tarbagatai, October 1864), which fixed a frontier in the Russian favour. The Chinese were thereby formally deprived of a belt of territory of some 350,000 square miles which, though certainly not effectively occupied by them, had equally certainly been claimed by the movements of their forward control-pickets. And in 1871, after seven years in which the Chinese inability to dislodge Yakub Beg had been displayed, the Russians took a further bite. In that year, ostensibly as a measure of order, they occupied Kuldja and its strategic upper valley of the Ili River.

In the usual sequence of Central Asian politics, the concern of other European powers for a stable balance now operated to restrain the Russian advance and support the Manchu authority. Peking's next military effort in Sinkiang was more successful, Yakub Beg was killed, and with British and French approval the Chinese not only reasserted their authority over the Muslim inhabitants, but in 1881 recovered the Ili salient from Russia. This took effect in the Treaty of St Petersburg (where it was signed), which Peking prefers to call the Treaty of Ili. Even so, it figures among the agreements listed by Mao Tse-tung's Government as unequal and revisable, since it still left in Russian hands the area of traditional Chinese pretensions beyond the mountains. Over the next twelve years, moreover, the boundary agreements that punctuated the slow process of demarcation exhibited a considerable amount of Russian nibbling.

There remained the southern extremities of the Sino-

Russian contact, where Sinkiang reached up from the Tarim basin into the lofty bastion of the Pamir. Here the frontier-question had a special character, partly determined by the encounter of Russian Imperial power with that of British India and its Kashmir dependency. Since the primary aim of British policy was to halt Russian penetration of the Pamir and to safeguard Kashmir from serving as an invasion-route to the Punjab, Peking had a diplomatic opportunity far beyond its actual strength for securing the south-western frontier of Sinkiang. An effective Chinese presence north of the Karakoram was clearly disclosed as a British objective, to be sealed by a tripartite settlement in the Pamir which should put a final term to Russian encroachment. Had the Chinese had the will to accept this unofficial alliance with British power, and the strength to assert themselves in frontier-contacts with Russia, they might have secured for Sinkiang not only an unambiguous western frontier, but also a southern frontier which would have retained for them the major part of that strategic bone of contention now grimly known as the Aksai Chin.*

The Chinese rejection of this opportunity was doubtless due in part to their instinctive reluctance towards treaty-making, especially during a phase of weakness; in part to preoccupations elsewhere (they were defeated by the Japanese in 1895); and in part to a cherished ambition to

* Of George Macartney, through whom persistent attempts were made to engage the Chinese in frontier-discussions, Dr Alistair Lamb has written: 'Of all the British diplomatists who dealt with China in the 19th century, there can have been none who managed more successfully to combine a deep loyalty to Britain with a genuine sympathy for, and understanding of, Chinese aims and ambitions. Alone in Kashgar, without at first official status and with no escort or other visible trappings of power, Macartney from 1890 until his retirement in 1918 virtually staved off the complete domination of Sinkiang by Russia' (*The China-India Border*, Chatham House, 1964).

extend their newly recovered hold in Sinkiang to the principality of Hunza at the western end of the Karakoram Range, over which both China and Kashmir claimed feudatory rights. The result, at all events, was that the British power, having failed in all attempts to secure Chinese participation, negotiated with Russia, in March 1895, an agreement in the Pamir which allotted to Afghanistan a narrow strip of territory (the Wakhan Valley) insulating their two empires from the direct contiguity which was seen as a danger to peace. The Chinese afterwards referred to this important agreement as a 'secret partition', and preserved in their maps a Chinese claim to the Wakhan Valley and an 'undelimited' status for the adjacent Sino-Russian frontier which should have been part and parcel of a tripartite settlement.

On the maps (whatever form of marking might be used) the long Central Asian frontier was thus established by the end of the 19th century; yet it represented neither a real division of power nor a barrier to movement. For the peoples of the area, with their homelands and grazing-grounds divided between two alien powers, the attempt to play off one against the other offered the best hope of preserving something of their own identity. The Chinese suppression of autonomy after the death of Yakub Beg had sent refugees into Russian Turkestan. Russian settlement on the Tsar's side of the border drove the dispossessed Kazakhs to revolt in 1916, and the Communist threat to their way of life after 1917 drove them to cross in large numbers to the Sinkiang side of their traditional homelands. Between 1931 and 1934 Muslim revolts against the Chinese and the proclamation of a Republic were only suppressed with the military assistance of the Russians, who used the occasion to complete their eco-

nomic domination of Sinkiang and to introduce Red
Army garrisons and propaganda-centres. In face of
Stalin's forced collectivization another 200,000 Kazakhs
moved into Sinkiang, where revolts against both Chinese
and Russians were bloodily defeated in 1936 and 1937.
In the north the Kazakhs of the Altai were in continuous
rebellion from 1940, and in 1946 an East Turkestan
Republic was once more proclaimed, no doubt with
Russian connivance, this time in the strategic Ili area
which Russia had long coveted and temporarily held.

The reconquest of Sinkiang by the Chinese Communists in 1949, which brought apparent stability to the
frontier, was prepared by Communist contacts inside
those organs of local administration which the Chinese
Nationalist Government had been compelled to concede.
But it could hardly have been effected, in the face of popular opinion, without the disconcerting factor of Soviet
assistance. In September 1949, before the proclamation of
the Chinese People's Republic and with Stalin maintaining to the last minute his official recognition of Chiang
Kai-shek's authority, Soviet air-transports flew advanced
units of Mao's Eighth Route Army into Urumchi, the
Sinkiang capital. Soviet indoctrination had broken local
efforts to consolidate a front of national resistance, and in
the Altai Soviet-trained Kazakhs were sent into action
against their fellow-countrymen. With the pincers now
closing from east and west, the next great Kazakh migration could only move south, in defiance of natural obstacles. A remnant survived the heroic journey across
Western Tibet into Kashmir, finally finding hospitality
in Turkey.

The ideological unity of former rivals, as expressed in
the 1950 Sino-Soviet Treaty of Friendship, Alliance and

Mutual Assistance, was not the only new factor injected into the history of the Central Asian borderlands. Equally important, and more enduring in its effects, was the Chinese adoption, for the first time, of a determined policy of colonial settlement, and of economic exploitation, in what was eventually designated the Sinkiang-Uighur Autonomous Region.

THE MONGOLIAN AREA

The greater part of China's northern frontier runs with Outer Mongolia, now the Mongolian People's Republic and was settled by agreement in December 1962. Yet it is difficult to believe that Chinese claims upon Outer Mongolia itself have been finally abandoned. It was Mao Tse-tung's expectation, according to a conversation with Edgar Snow in July 1936, that 'when the people's revolution has been victorious in China, the Outer Mongolian Republic will automatically become a part of the Chinese

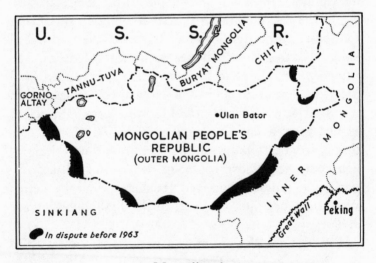

2. Mongolian Area

federation, at their own will'. When he made this statement a fictional Chinese sovereignty over Outer Mongolia
had not been formally broken, although its Communist
Government was subservient to Moscow and there was
not even a Chinese representative in Ulan Bator. But
before Mao Tse-tung's victory in China, Stalin secured
from the KMT Government, in 1945, an agreement for
Chinese recognition of the independence of the Mongolian Republic.

After coming to power the Chinese Communists
evidently decided that there was more to be gained by
promoting Sino-Mongolian relations on this independent
basis than by challenging it. As the fruits of 'leaning to
one side', the gain of control in Sinkiang could be balanced
against the loss of title in Mongolia, where the opportunity to exchange diplomatic, cultural and economic missions was quickly accepted. The whole question of Outer
Mongolian autonomy, however, derives historically from
agreements concluded with Russia by the Chinese Republic
after the overthrow of the Ch'ing (Manchu) dynasty. And
the term 'unequal', previously applied in China to treaty-
concessions made to other powers during the last half-
century of the Manchu Empire, was extended by the very
deliberate *People's Daily* article of 8 March 1963, to cover
any losses of 'Chinese territory in the North, South, East
or West', during 'the hundred years or so prior to the
victory of the Chinese revolution'. The Chinese policy
was said to be the peaceful settlement of any outstanding
issues 'when conditions are ripe', until which time 'the
status quo should be maintained'.

The case of Mongolia, as it happens, offers an earlier
example of the time appearing ripe for the Chinese
Government to revoke unilaterally a previous agreement

and extend its control to a 'lost' frontier. It was in alliance with the Mongols that the Manchus had conquered China in the 17th century, producing in turn a Chinese Imperial claim to the Mongolian lands. In the last years of the Ch'ing dynasty at the turn of the present century, the Outer Mongolian movement to regain independence was a reaction against the increasing pressure of Chinese colonization, northward from Inner Mongolia. The movement was supported by the Tsarist Russian Government, to which it turned for aid. Intervention was seen to be in Russia's interest, but it was equally in Russia's interest to ensure that full independence from both powers should not result. When the Manchu Empire was overthrown from within in 1911 Outer Mongolia (like Tibet) proclaimed its independence, which by Russian mediation in 1913 it was compelled to reduce to 'autonomy', with suzerainty for the Chinese Republic and openings for penetration by Russia. In 1917, however, the Tsarist Government was itself overthrown by revolution. The time was ripe for the Chinese to send troops into Outer Mongolia and cancel its autonomy, which they did by Presidential decree in November 1919.

Eighteen months later they were expelled by the forces of the White Russian Baron Unghern-Sternberg, acting and accepted as a Mongolian liberator. No sooner had autonomy been restored to Outer Mongolia than the Red Army, with Mongolian Communists from Soviet territory, crossed the border, destroyed the Government, shot Baron Unghern-Sternberg and established Outer Mongolia as the first Soviet satellite.

The right which the Chinese Communists have reserved to re-examine, among other past agreements, the 1864 Treaty of Chuguchak, could be used to reopen the question of a former Mongolian territory of the Manchu Empire which is now part of the Soviet Union. This was the 80,000 square miles of Urianghai in the North-West. The Treaty of Chuguchak, though mainly concerned with the Sino-Russian frontier in Turkestan, also referred to the northern frontier of Outer Mongolia as dividing the Chinese Empire from Russian territory. And Urianghai, as later admitted in Moscow, was there defined as within the Chinese dominions. In 1911, in support of the Outer Mongolian autonomists, Russian forces entered by this route and occupied Urianghai, which in 1914 was detached as a Russian protectorate. It was nominally and briefly recovered when Chinese troops returned to Outer Mongolia after the Russian Revolution, but the Russians were back again in 1922 when the Red Army brought a Communist régime to Outer Mongolia. This time Urianghai became the 'Tuvinian People's Republic' and then the 'Republic of Tannu Tuva', which in 1926 entered into mutual recognition of independence with the Mongolian People's Republic. Independence in both cases was at Soviet disposal, and in 1944 Tannu Tuva—with an area of 64,000 square miles, a population of 70,000 and considerable natural resources—was quietly incorporated in the Soviet Union as an Autonomous Region (later raised in status to Autonomous Republic.) Chinese Communist maps apparently accept this loss, but the claim is preserved in maps issued by the Chinese Nationalist Government in Taiwan. Despite the concession of Outer Mongolian independence extracted from Chiang Kai-shek by Stalin in 1945, the Chinese frontiers on these maps enclose Outer Mongolia as a province and Tannu Tuva as a division of it.

That the boundary between Inner and Outer Mongolia

has become the frontier of the Chinese People's Republic for 2,500 miles is a result of Russian power and policy, both Tsarist and Soviet, not of Mongolian rights and aspirations. Intervening as mediator in 1913 between the Outer Mongolian nationalists and the Chinese KMT Republic, Russia in 1915 brought the parties to a tripartite agreement with provision for formal delimitation by a tripartite boundary commission. In the meantime a 'frontier zone' was provisionally indicated. The First World War and the Russian Revolution interrupted the process of fixing the frontier, which was shown on Chinese Communist maps as undetermined. Soviet and most other maps, however, indicated a fixed international boundary.

THE MANCHURIAN AREA

China's frontier with the Soviet Far East runs for some 2,000 miles, from the mountainous north-east corner of the Mongolian People's Republic to the Pacific Ocean south of Vladivostok. It is a physical boundary, following the Amur river-system: in the first 600 miles it is that of the tributary Argun, then of the Amur itself eastwards until it receives the Ussuri from the south. Here the boundary turns southwards and runs upstream to the headwaters of the Ussuri, whence a relatively short sector links the watershed with the coast.

The general case for natural frontiers has been criticized in Chinese Communist publications; and this important area of the Soviet Far East, carrying the Trans-Siberian Railway to Vladivostok, represents historically a very considerable invasion of the former Manchu Empire. With the establishment of the Chinese People's Government the impression of a stabilized frontier, however, had been strengthened by the 1956 agreement for joint

Sino-Soviet investigation and development of the Amur
River Basin, and co-operation in subsequent operations
did not appear to have been interrupted by worsening
relations and the withdrawal of Soviet technicians from

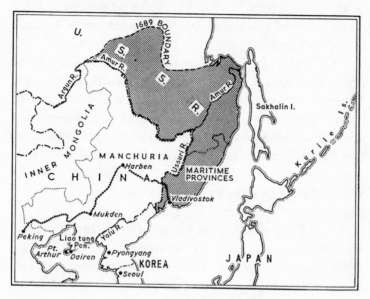

3. Manchurian Area

China. In normally current maps only one point of discrepancy was observed, near the Soviet city of Khabarovsk. Here the Chinese claimed an island at the Amur-
Ussuri confluence, which in Soviet maps was included on
the Russian side.

Maps of Chinese irredenta were a different matter. The
loss of 'China's Great North-East' to which Liu Pei-
Hua's *Brief History of Modern China* had drawn attention
was apparently fully redressed for the purpose of a
brochure distributed at the Chinese Trade Fair in Mexico
(December 1963–January 1964). In this a map of the

47

world picked out in special tone the territories of Mexico and China, with the latter clearly covering the old imperial lands east and north of the rivers. Moreover, three of the 'unequal treaties' challenged by the *People's Daily* in March 1963, were those in which the possession of these lands had been secured to Russia. These were the Treaties of Aigun, Tientsin and Peking.

The Treaty of Aigun (May 1858) established the Amur River as a frontier between north and south, involving a Chinese surrender to Russia of about 185,000 square miles. A form of Chinese jurisdiction, however, was allowed over the Manchu inhabitants of what were called the 'Sixty-Four Settlements' on the left bank of the Amur. East of the Ussuri the maritime lands facing the Pacific were to be common to Russia and China pending a future decision on the matter.

The Treaty of Tientsin (June 1858) followed closely upon the Aigun Treaty and settled commercial matters. It further provided for the survey of frontiers, although this had already been covered in the preceding settlement.

The Treaty of Peking (November 1860) sealed the fate of the territories between the Ussuri and the Pacific (133,000 square miles) which were ceded to Russia. The frontier was established as running south along the Ussuri, and thence to the boundary of Korea, with provision for surveying and mapping this sector.

The first treaty concerning this area, however, dates from as early as 1689. The Treaty of Nerchinsk of that year was indeed the first ever to be concluded between the Chinese Empire and a Western Power. The beginning of a purposive Russian penetration east of Lake Baikal had coincided roughly with the establishment of the Manchu dynasty in 1644. But before turning south to the conquest of China the Manchus had extended their native control northwards over the Amur Basin, and the predatory Cossack occupation of the valley in the next few years came up against, and defeated, a Manchu-Chinese force. The Nerchinsk Treaty of 1689 followed a period of Russian efforts to make diplomatic contact with Peking and of Chinese efforts to dislodge them from their new strongpoints and settlements. It gained for the Russians commercial openings in the Celestial Empire. But the Manchu negotiators, supported by preponderant military forces, achieved a frontier-settlement along the watershed range between the valleys of the Lena and the Amur, thus retaining the latter and requiring the removal of Russian settlements and the destruction of their fort at Albazin.

Despite discrepancies in the different texts of the treaty on the subject of undecided territories, the Nerchinsk settlement was not seriously disturbed during the next century and a half. But the Manchus failed to consolidate their position, since their own movements were directed southwards at the same time as they discouraged Chinese settlement in the Manchurian lands. New contacts and communications were put to far better use by the penetrating Russians than by the exclusive Chinese, and by the 1850's the decline of China's imperial power had removed most of the obstacles to Russia's advance in this region— the only one where she had a clear advantage over rival Western Powers. The Russian strategy which pushed the frontier southwards to the Amur River with the 'unequal treaties' of Aigun and Tientsin in 1858 was thus able to combine physical occupation with a diplomatic presentation of Russia to the Chinese as an ally against their other despoilers.

The even more valuable maritime provinces east of the Ussuri were secured by Russia two years later in different circumstances. In 1859 the Imperial Court at Peking, blindly over-estimating initial successes in resisting Anglo-French demands, was more inclined to remind the Russians of past treaty-obligations than to depend on their assurances of assistance. The Russians therefore courted the Western Allies, who in August 1860 were on the one hand advancing upon Peking, and on the other defending Shanghai for the Chinese authorities against the Tai-ping rebels. The Chinese were not deceived by the tactics of the Russians, whom indeed they believed to be responsible for inciting the other barbarians. But they were defeated. When the Ussuri territory was surrendered in the Sino-Russian Treaty of Peking in November 1860, the site and name of the Russian port of Vladivostok ('Dominion of the East') had already been chosen.

In 1891 construction of the Vladivostok–Khabarovsk section of the Russian Trans-Siberian Railway was begun; and in 1895 Russia—this time in the rôle of China's protector against Japan—secured permission to build a railway-link with Vladivostok inside the Chinese frontier, across Manchuria. This was followed by further concessions, including mineral rights and the leases of Port Arthur and Dairen. By defeating Russia in 1905 Japan secured these rights for herself, but a subsequent *détente* defined 'spheres of influence' in the Manchurian region for both Russia and Japan. The arrangement produced the so-called 'Kuropatkin Line' along the 43rd parallel, which was apparently seen in Moscow as the basis for an eventual north–south boundary between Russian and Chinese Asia. Extended westwards to the Tien-Shan, it would have claimed for Russia, besides Northern Manchuria, the whole of Outer Mongolia and the northern portion of Sinkiang.

Secret agreements between Moscow and Tokyo, as allies in the First World War, for co-operation in defence of their 'vital interests' in the Far East were, of course, invalidated by the Russian Revolution in 1917. But the apparent renunciation of Tsarist acquisitions in the Far East by the Karakhan Declaration (25 July 1919) took a significantly different turn in the following year, when 'the entire territory of the former Russian Empire, east of the River Selenga and Lake Baikal' was transferred, none of it to China, but all of it to a newly declared 'Far Eastern Republic' with a very large measure of independence. Japanese troops were advancing into the power-vacuum offered by the collapse of Tsarist Russia, and Moscow's urgent need was for a policy that might unite Bolshevik and anti-Bolshevik inhabitants in a nationalist preservation of the territory. The Japanese withdrew from the mainland, and three weeks later, on 14 November 1922, the Republic was absorbed into the central Soviet State as the Far Eastern Territory of the RSFSR (later reconstituted as the Khabarovsk and Maritime Territories). Declarations defining its boundaries made no departure from the frontier established with China during the Tsarist period. Beyond the frontier, 'all the rights of the former Russian Empire in the zone of the Chinese Eastern Railway' had already been claimed on behalf of the short-lived 'Far Eastern Republic'.* But these, in the course of events, fell to the Japanese, pushing forward with increasing force the undeclared war between their

* The Karakhan Declaration had specifically undertaken that this Chinese Eastern Railway should be handed over to the Chinese without compensation. A Russian pretence that this was a forged interpellation has been disproved.

'special rights' in Manchuria and the rising substance and spirit of Chinese nationalism. Such disputes of the Amur River frontier as occurred thus involved Russia and Japan, or the Soviet Union and the puppet régimes which the Japanese, following the Soviet precedent, proceeded to establish in North China.

In the agreement reached with the Kuomintang Government of China in May 1924, the Soviet Government as we have seen, had avoided any undertaking pointing to a frontier-rectification in favour of China. In 1945 the Government of Chiang Kai-shek was again in too weak a position to obtain from Stalin's USSR, in the Treaty of Friendship and Alliance, anything more than a profession of mutual Russian and Chinese respect for each other's sovereignty and territorial integrity. Up till the success of the Chinese Communists, indeed, the prospects were rather of the advance of Soviet power south of the Amur (as well as in Sinkiang). And Stalin's double stratagem of stripping the Manchurian industries on the one hand, and allowing arms to fall into Communist Chinese hands on the other, strongly suggests the aim of prolonging conflict in the coveted area and crippling its winners. Mao Tse-tung's rapid advance to central power transformed the situation on the Chinese side of the existing frontier. It secured a slow liquidation of the Russian extra-territorial advantages which had been yielded to Japan but were re-assigned to Stalin by his Western Allies at Yalta in anticipation of victory. Of these China had by 1952 recovered the Chinese Eastern (Changchun) Railway without compensation, but the pretext of the Korean War served to keep Soviet forces in Port Arthur. Only after Stalin's death was China's re-possession within the Manchurian frontiers completed by the Soviet withdrawal from Port Arthur in 1955 and the transfer to China of Soviet shares in the Manchurian joint-stock companies.

On the frontier itself, and Chinese claims beyond it, official silence was complete. Even in Mao's earlier and ambitious territorial aims, as expressed to Edgar Snow in 1936, what was to be recovered in this area had been 'all territories lost to Japanese imperialism'. In a Communist programme no claims against the Soviet Union could be admitted. And their revival in March 1963 followed an ideological campaign in which the title of the Soviet leadership to be regarded as genuinely Communist had been progressively impugned.

III

THE QUESTION OF TIBET

As in the case of Outer Mongolia, Chinese relations with Tibet involve two separate considerations of boundary-matters. The first applies to the frontiers between China proper and the territory over which a form of suzerainty is claimed or exercised. The second, which applies to the frontiers of the territory with other States, arises only if it falls under sufficient control to be considered as a part of China. In April 1912, the announced intention of the new Chinese Republic was to convert the lands of the Mongols and the Tibetans into Chinese Provinces, on the lines of the 'New Dominion' declared in Sinkiang after the destruction of the native principality of Yakub Beg. Russian power, as we have noted, prevented the execution of this project in Outer Mongolia, and prevents it to this day. In the case of Tibet British power in 1912 compelled the new Chinese Republic to recall the military expedition which had already been despatched. At the same time a British recognition of Chinese suzerainty in Tibet was made conditional on a Chinese recognition that suzerainty did not include the right to intervene in the country's internal administration or the right to send in military forces. The Chinese avoided any guarantee of this kind, but offered as conciliatory gestures permission for the Dalai Lama to return from the exile in India forced upon him by the Manchu invasion of 1910, and the restoration of his official rank. In fact the Dalai Lama had already returned to Lhasa and resumed the temporal and spiritual government, and he replied that he wanted no rank or appointment from Peking.

In the Tibetan view the formal relationship with China had been brought to an end. The turning-point had come in 1910, when the last spasms of the Manchu Empire found a capable and ruthless general, Chao Er-feng, and an expedition equipped with modern weapons, to carry invasion to Lhasa itself—the first time that the Chinese had entered the capital against the Tibetan will. Tibetan independence, declared in reaction to this aggression, was made good when the collapse of the Manchu régime allowed the Tibetans to expel the invaders from the entire country, killing the commander. Defence of the frontier against further Chinese attacks continued until 1913, and the Simla Conference of October 1913 to April 1914, was called by Britain, acting in an essentially mediatory rôle, to define the relationship and frontiers of two parties conferring with equal status, and then to clarify its own position. On the results of the Simla Conference the International Commission of Jurists reported in 1960 the following findings by its Legal Inquiry Committee on Tibet:

In the original scheme of things, according to one of the notes exchanged between the plenipotentiaries, 'It is understood by the high contracting parties that "Thibet" forms part of Chinese territory.'

Great Britain and Tibet were thus originally prepared to agree that Tibet was part of Chinese territory, but was autonomous under Chinese suzerainty. The Chinese refusal to sign the Convention meant quite simply that Great Britain and Tibet agreed to withhold the recognition of suzerainty, and with it the understanding that Tibet was part of Chinese territory. *Vis-à-vis* Tibet China was thus faced with a reversion to the *status quo*, namely the proclamation of Tibet's independence in 1912 by the Thirteenth

Dalai Lama, with the expulsion of the Chinese from Tibet in the same year.*

In consequence Tibet continued to exercise *de facto* and *de jure* independence from China, and with Britain and British India an agreed relationship which was also basically independent. British influence in the area was withdrawn in 1947, her treaty-rights in Tibet being transferred to the independent Government of India. A Tibetan delegation was on its way to China to negotiate a new relationship when in 1950 the Chinese Communist Government initiated the forced integration of Tibet with the Chinese People's Republic. This had direct consequences in both categories of frontier-question.

THE TIBET–CHINA BOUNDARIES

Political Tibet has been defined by Mr H. E. Richardson, the last British and first Indian Head of Mission in Lhasa, as the area (some half-million square miles) in which 'Tibetan Governments ruled continuously from the earliest times down to 1951'. Northwards and eastwards of this area is a large belt of territory—in Tsinghai and Szechwan—which has been ethnographically Tibetan from a remote age, though Chinese population-policies have by now affected the racial balance. Beyond this again and on all sides, north, south, east and west, the radiation of influence from Lhasa was at one time very considerable. At its greatest extent, between the 6th and 8th centuries A.D., it reached the oases of the northern trade-route from Hami to Samarkand, the Yellow River and the middle reaches of the Yangtse, and over the Himalayan passes to the lower Brahmaputra and the Ganges.

* *Tibet and the Chinese People's Republic*. Geneva, 1960.

Vague and remote as this kind of spiritual suzerainty may be, it can still be resuscitated where Tibetan traditions are required to support a modern Chinese claim on the international map. When the Sino-Tibetan boundary, however, was under discussion at the Simla Conference, the Chinese delegate, Ivan Chen, denied any political

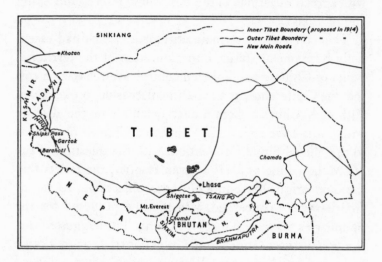

4. Tibet

validity to Tibetan ecclesiastical jurisdiction. 'What the Dalai Lama exercises,' he protested on 7 March 1914, 'is only spiritual influence and not temporal authority.... The sphere within which spiritual influence is extended can under no circumstances be claimed as the extent of his temporal authority.'

The Tibetan 'asking-price' at Simla in the matter of her boundary with China was undoubtedly exaggerated. The Chinese reply was to demand, as against Tibet's assertion of independence, the recognition of full Chinese sovereignty, which would have left boundary-questions virtually at Peking's disposal.* The British search for a compromise lay first in linking the concept of Chinese 'suzerainty' firmly with that of Tibetan 'autonomy'. And then in the proposition—on a largely theoretical analogy with Inner and Outer Mongolia—of an 'Inner Tibet' (Sino-Tibetan marches) and an 'Outer Tibet' (Tibet proper) with agreed variations in the controlling interest of Peking and of Lhasa.

This converted the main argument, which had essentially been one of status, into a question of the territorial limits of Chinese and Tibetan control. And it was on this that the Conference, as a tripartite discussion, broke down. Although Chinese Communist polemics in the dispute with India have repeatedly connected Chinese objections to the 'illegal Simla Convention' with the question of the McMahon Line as a Himalayan frontier, the fact is that the sole original ground of those objections, so far as frontiers were concerned, was the line proposed for the boundaries between Tibet and China. The suggested distinction between 'Inner' and 'Outer Tibet', though it came to be indicated on some Western maps, never achieved any meaning. Tibet's *de facto* boundary, in the area of Chinese pressure from the east, was effectively held on the Yangtse line, leaving most of the 'Inner Tibet' periphery and its largely Tibetan population in Chinese Szechwan (Sikang). On the north-east the *de facto* boundary left a considerable part of both 'Inner' and 'Outer' Tibet in China's possession. Within these limits, however, the Lhasa Government exercised full authority until the

* This claim was rested upon the 13th-century operations of the Mongol Chinghiz Khan and his successors, despite the fact that their effective overlordship of Tibet *preceded* the completion of their conquest of China, and had been reduced to a formality by a Tibetan national revival before the Chinese themselves threw off the Mongol dynasty.

Chinese Communist invasion and the ensuing 17-Point Sino-Tibetan Agreement of 1951.

The Chinese repudiation of the Simla Convention, and of the map accepted and signed by their own as well as the other two plenipotentiaries, was a measure of their unfulfilled ambitions. Yet the agreement that had been sought was in no sense extortionate. The McMahon map of the Sino-Tibetan boundaries was an obvious compromise, in which, had it been implemented, the Tibetans stood to surrender to Chinese influence, as 'Inner Tibet', areas in the east from which they had already dislodged their invaders. And if the legal formulation of 'suzerainty' which was also offered at Simla failed to recognize a Chinese right to convert Tibet into a province, it certainly proposed a restriction of Tibetan independence which Lhasa disliked and Peking was powerless to impose. When all attempts to obtain Chinese assent had failed, the alternative was demonstrated by Tibet's unfettered exercise of its internal and external functions as a State—beginning with the bilateral Anglo-Tibetan agreement which settled the frontier between Tibet and India (at that time including Burma).

THE PARTITION OF TIBET

Before the liquidation of the last Manchu adventure in Tibet, General Chao Er-feng had proposed to the Imperial Government the establishment of a new Chinese province, Sikang, to extend from inside Szechwan on the west, over a very large area of Tibet to within a short distance of Lhasa. After the collapse of the Empire the Chinese Government was powerless to give these ideas of partition any substance. But they found their way into a number of maps, not all of them Chinese. In 1928 there were signs of a revival of the project by the Kuomintang Government, which in practice used the mythical extent of a Chinese province as cover for any penetrations which could be made. These may have owed as much to the independent ambitions of Szechwan Governors as to the administration in Nanking, which early in 1932 concluded an armistice with Lhasa. This was immediately followed, to Tibetan indignation, by a further attack from Szechwan and an advance to threaten Chamdo. On an appeal from Tibet, British pressure produced a cease-fire in September 1932, but in 1943 the Governor of Sikang was one of those ordered by Chiang Kai-shek to move troops to the Tibetan border.

After the establishment of the Chinese People's Republic the name Sikang dropped out of use, except for the new east–west Sikang–Tibet Highway (not to be confused with the west–east Sinkiang–Tibet Highway) constructed in 1954. Formal abolition of the Sikang Province was announced in July 1955, but Peking had already put into effect a different partition of Tibet.

The 17-Point Agreement which the Chinese Communists extorted from Tibet in 1951 under military pressure made no reference to boundaries between 'the Tibet Region' and China. Stubbornly debated as the question might have been in 1913–14, the frontier was never the main concern of Chinese policy, which aimed at the exercise of power beyond it. When that aim had been secured by force, discussion of boundaries became irrelevant. Thus although (in the words of the International Jurists' Report) 'there is nothing in the 17–Point Agreement to suggest that Tibet was to be carved up', the Chinese consulted their own administrative convenience in dividing the country into three parts, only one of which remained, and that nominally, under the jurisdiction of the Dalai Lama and his Cabinet. When the last vestiges of this jurisdiction were obliterated in the Chinese action against the Tibetan rising in 1959, the division no longer had a purpose to serve and appears to have lapsed.

One alteration effected by Chinese maps and statements concerning the Tibet Region and its frontiers deserves notice. In so far as a historical claim existed to the West Aksai Chin area of Ladakh, or to some part of it, it had previously been made on behalf of Tibet, with which that high and desolate plateau has a geographical connection. After occupying the area, however, the Chinese Communists incorporated it, not in Tibet but in Sinkiang, thereafter shifting the basis of their arguments as best they could when challenged by India on evidence.

IV

A NEW CHINA ON THE
FRONTIERS: 1950-5

THE YALU RIVER: FRONTIER OR SEMI-FRONTIER?

THE peninsula of Korea, with its long history of an autonomous civilization and its single and unchanging land-frontier along the Yalu and Tuman Rivers, offered with the defeat of Japan in 1945 a clear-cut case for liberation from alien imperialism. In 1910 Japan had annexed Korea as a colonial territory by unilateral declaration, having obtained protectorate powers in the country five years earlier as a result of the Russo-Japanese War. Before that, though suffering at different periods Mongol, Japanese and Manchu invasions, the Koreans had preserved a racial and national entity, accepting cultural influences but also exerting them upon their neighbours. Traditional concepts of dependence towards the Chinese Empire were kept alive during the 19th century more by the diplomacy of Korean rulers in resistance to Western approaches than by the Chinese themselves, who declined to be answerable as a controlling Power.

After 1876, however, when Japan and Korea concluded a treaty on trade and intercourse on terms of sovereign equality, Peking had begun to assert a stronger position, encouraged by American and other Western requests for Chinese 'good offices' in relation to this important region. For a few years Korea's course did appear to have been diverted from prospects of independence in its modern form to those of Chinese protectorate status. This in turn served to present Japan as a bulwark for Korea against both China and Russia, and the Sino-Japanese war of 1894–5 compelled the Chinese to recognize the 'full and complete independence' of Korea as well as ceding to Japan Formosa (Taiwan), the Pescadores Islands and the Liaotung Peninsula in South Manchuria. Fifteen years later Korea was a Japanese colony.

The 1895 Treaty of Shimonoseki is one of the 'unequal treaties' specifically challenged by the Chinese Communists in the *People's Daily* article of March 1963. So far as Japanese sovereignty in Taiwan, the islands or the Chinese mainland was concerned the treaty had, of course, been completely nullified by 1945. To revive it as an existing grievance was, therefore, to throw some doubt upon present Chinese attitudes towards the full and complete independence of Korea.

In Mao Tse-tung's sketch of territorial aims thirteen years before he achieved central power (as recorded by Edgar Snow, 1936) Korea and Taiwan had both been placed in a special category. Both were to be given 'enthusiastic help' if their peoples expressed a wish to throw off Japanese imperialist rule. In the event they were liberated without Mao's participation. The only difficulties in the way of Korean independence under the guarantee of Allied victory stemmed from rival Russian and Chinese (KMT) ambitions. Chiang Kai-shek was in a relatively weak position, as was only too clear in the conduct of Allied conferences. Stalin, with a Soviet declaration of war against Japan as a bargaining-counter, was in a strong one.

A free and independent Korea 'in due course', announced as a war aim by Roosevelt, Churchill and Chiang at Cairo in November 1943, was afterwards endorsed by

Stalin. But final *de jure* disposal of international questions involving Japan awaited peace-treaties which neither Russia nor China have yet negotiated. The *de facto* position in Korea, as it faced the Chinese People's Republic on its establishment on 1 October 1949, was mainly the result of a new feature in the history of this area. In 1945 Russian forces, estimated at some 200,000, had for the first time crossed the northern frontier into Korea, under the Yalta agreement, in the week of Russian beligerence before the Japanese surrender. By the end of 1948 the Soviet troops were said to have been withdrawn, and a few months later the much smaller U.S. forces were evacuated from the southern half of the country, where a Korean Republic was then inaugurated after elections supervised and certified by a Commission of the United Nations. The formation of a rival People's Government in the north, composed of Russian-trained Communists, followed almost immediately.

The only interested party to which this confused and dangerous situation appeared to offer nothing was China: unless, that is, China were prepared to accept a fully independent Korea under the auspices of a United Nations in which American interests were powerful. Had Mao been able to choose this course he could not only have secured China's frontier on the Yalu and Tuman Rivers, but in all probability a U.N. seat for his Government and a free hand in Taiwan as well. The directives of Chinese Communist policy at this time must therefore be sought within the general strategy of 'leaning to one side'. And however much or little of Stalin's intentions in regard to Korea may have been divulged to Mao during the secret conversations of 1949–50, the North Korean invasion of the Korean Republic in June 1950, with Soviet armaments using a supply-line to which the Chinese were chronically sensitive, must have been viewed with mixed feelings from Peking. Only with the rolling back of this attack, and with victory throughout the peninsula on the point of falling to the forces of the United Nations, was massive Chinese intervention ordered. And thus, when a situation of North-South stalemate in Korea was stabilized after the death of Stalin, China could appear to have been concerned mainly and successfully with the defence of her proper frontier.

Of this frontier-line between Korea and China there has never been any substantial argument. The question is only as to the degree or kind of power which China, or in certain circumstances Russia, could exercise beyond it. There is, however, one locality of disagreement. The mountain of Paektu San, from the slopes of which the Yalu and the Tuman flow respectively west and east to delineate the boundary, has been claimed in maps and statements by both China and Korea, with some indication of Soviet support for the latter. As distinct from the Sino-Nepalese competition for the possession of Mount Everest, the area in question on the Sino-Korean frontier has been assigned economic value by Chinese prospecting-teams.

HIMALAYA AND KARAKORAM

Military action in Tibet was initiated by the Chinese in October 1950, when the Communist invaders of South Korea had been driven back to the 38th parallel. The preference for a forced rather than a negotiated settlement of the Tibetan question suggests that the Chinese gave high priority to their planned military connections (a matter on which Lhasa was traditionally stubborn) with Sinkiang in the west. Chinese authority had always been hampered by the length and weakness of its communications with Sinkiang, whose inhabitants were even less disposed to welcome a Chinese Communist régime than they had been to submit to the rule of imperial Peking.

The 'resolved policy' of the Central People's Government was not only to 'liberate' Tibet but also to 'defend the frontiers of China'. The formidable (and therefore hitherto unmilitarized) mountain-boundaries which this policy would activate extended for 2,500 miles, from the sensitive 'meeting-point of three empires' at the Pamir Knot to the tribal frontier-zone of northern Burma. Without considering the Sinkiang-Soviet border, the Chinese move into Tibet was thus to concern, from west to east, the following neighbour-States.

(i) *Afghanistan* (Wakhan Valley salient in the Pamir).

(ii) *Pakistan* (*de facto* responsibility, in unsettled Kashmir dispute, for frontier eastward to Karakoram Pass).

(iii) *India* (Ladakh, Punjab, Himachal Pradesh, Uttar Pradesh).

(iv) *Nepal* (independent).

(v) and (vi) *India* (responsible by treaties for defence of *Sikkim* and *Bhutan*).

(vii) *India* (North-East Frontier Agency, administered by Central Government acting through Assam Governor).

(viii) *Burma* (northern frontier-zone).

In the mountain-areas mapped by British surveyors during the 19th century, watersheds were frequently found to represent a natural and traditionally accepted frontier. Nor can it be disputed that the watershed-line was a sensible basis for the McMahon frontier defined in 1913–14 as separating Tibet from India and Burma. In a general description of the southern frontiers of Chinese power, however, the watershed-principle is significant only when allowance has been made for the great complexities of the terrain and for three facts in particular: that the alignment of highest peaks is not always or necessarily that of a main watershed; that the Himalayan range constitutes the rim of the Tibetan plateau rather than a barrier between two plains; and that in the western sector it disappears as one of the more southerly ridges in a vast mountain-corrugation of which the northern edge is formed by the Karakoram.

The historical conditions governing the frontier in the national sectors that have just been enumerated are no less complex under detailed examination. But they may be summarized in their essentials.

(i) and (ii) The lofty Pamir-Karakoram line, which was to concern *Afghanistan* and *Pakistan* (as well as India), had at one time appeared so naturally impenetrable that for forty years after the creation of the State of Jammu and Kashmir in 1846 British policy was able to leave matters of frontier-control largely to the Kashmir Government. The latter claimed, but had difficulty in exercising, feudatory authority over the mountain-chiefdoms of Gilgit, Hunza, Nagar and others of the Upper Indus, and in this the paramount British power was reluctant to interfere unless lawlessness endangered the slender trade-routes or invited foreign intervention. As we have seen (Chapter III) this attitude was changed after 1890 by the apparently menacing advance of Russian power, producing a more direct British relationship with the border-principalities and a virtual, though one-sided, alliance with the weakened Chinese Empire. The eventual Anglo-Russian agreement of 1895 on the Pamir boundaries, with its wedge of 'neutral' territory, produced a frontier of about fifty miles between Afghanistan and Chinese Sinkiang. This the Chinese continued to regard, along with the rest of the Pamir settlement, as invalid and secretly arrived at.

By 1950, as a result of the Indo-Pakistani difference in Kashmir, *de facto* responsibility for the frontier from the Pamir junction eastwards to the Karakoram Pass was in the hands of Pakistan, the local Muslim chiefs having refused allegiance to the Kashmir Maharajah on his accession to India. Aside from some earlier Hunza claims to grazing-grounds north of the watershed, which British-Indian policy had for a time tended to support, the natural boundary along the Karakoram Range had found practical agreement, though without a settlement. Extensions of the Kashmir border north of the Karakoram, which appeared (and still appear) on a number of widely-used maps, had no official British sanction after 1927, and have had none in the maps of independent India.

(iii) Buttressing the Karakoram on the east, the Kun Lun range encloses a desolate area of high plateau where Buddhist *Ladakh* marches with Sinkiang on the north and Tibet on the east. Two treaties confirmed Ladakh's frontier as 'anciently established', though without further definition. The first dated from 1684,* when Ladakh was a major Himalayan kingdom, and the second from 1842, after its subjection by Gulab Singh, himself a feudatory of the Sikh Empire. In making over the semi-independent State of Kashmir to Gulab Singh and his heirs in 1846, the British-Indian authorities hoped at the same time to

* According to the *Indian Official Report* of 1961. Cunningham's *Ladak* (1954) dated the treaty 1687, and Alastair Lamb's Chatham House Essay of 1964 dates it 1683.

negotiate a fixed frontier with Tibet and the Chinese Empire in this area and to create conditions for peaceful trade. When it proved impossible to draw Tibet and China into discussion, frontier-survey and definition were carried out by British officers, who adopted for this purpose a principle of 'watershed lines between the drainages of different rivers'. Knowledge of the natural features of the inaccessible northern plateau (Aksai Chin) still lacked accuracy; but southwards from the Lanak Pass and through the Pangong Lake area the years of careful survey culminated (*Kashmir Atlas*, 1868) in a well-authenticated boundary which held good until the Chinese Communist challenge. As the frontier of Kashmir the boundary became a responsibility of independent India with the accession of the Maharajah of Kashmir in 1947, and the subsequent dispute with Pakistan left this eastern area of Kashmir on the Indian side of the cease-fire line.

From Kashmir to Nepal the Tibetan boundary was that of the former British India, which covered the small states of the upper Sutlej and the territories of Garwhal and Kumaon (U.P.). The latter, coming under British administration in 1816 in the termination of Gurkha encroachments on their neighbours, had given British India its first direct frontier with Tibet, in a stretch of the high Himalayan watershed of special significance for trade and pilgrimage over the passes.

(iv) *Nepal*, a tributary of the Chinese Empire from 1792 to 1816, came under British Indian protection in that year after the Gurkha War, but retained links with Tibet and, by a Nepalese-Tibetan agreement of 1856, special representation and privileges. It also continued to send a formal five-yearly tribute-mission to Peking until 1908, but broke off the connection with the fall of the

Manchu Empire in 1911. Occupying 56,000 square miles of mountainous country on the southern side of the main watershed, and dominated by a Hindu culture and dynasty, Nepal had also commercial and military relations with India; but under British guarantee and with a British Resident its independence was respected to such an extent that it could remain virtually a closed country. Mao Tse-tung's view of Nepal as a territory of which China had been robbed by 'unequal treaties' was expressed as early as 1939 (*Chinese Revolution and the Chinese Communist Party*).

The independent Government of India inherited existing British-Indian diplomatic relations with Nepal, but fresh treaties, one of peace and friendship and the other commercial, were signed between India and Nepal on 31 January 1950. Shortly afterwards, on 17 March, the Indian Prime Minister said in Parliament: 'It is not possible for the Indian Government to tolerate any violation of Nepal from anywhere, even though there is no military alliance between the two countries. Any possible invasion of Nepal . . . would immediately involve the safety of India.' In the same speech Nehru said that the Indian Government had advised the Government of Nepal 'in all earnestness, to bring themselves into line with democratic forces that are striving in the world today'. Indian influence and encouragement were apparent in the revolutionary change which terminated the domination of the Nepalese Rana family in the latter part of the same year. This took place at the same time as the Chinese invasion of Tibet.

(v) On the eastern flank of Nepal, the small but important state of *Sikkim*, a British-Indian protectorate by the treaty of 1817, had the distinction of a Chinese recognition of its status and its frontier. The 1890 Anglo-

Chinese Convention which secured this was also, however, an illustration of the historic difficulty of reaching a settlement involving both Peking and Lhasa. The British policy on this occasion of gratifying the Chinese desire for a show of 'suzerainty' had the effect of ensuring that no Tibetan ratification of the Sikkim-Tibet frontier would be obtainable.

Independent India's relations with Sikkim were confirmed in December 1950 by a treaty under which Sikkim remained a protectorate in respect of foreign relations and defence. With responsibility for Sikkim's territorial integrity, the Indian Government retained the right to construct and maintain communications and take such military measures as it considered necessary. So far as concerned relations with China, the 1890 Convention and the joint frontier-demarcation of 1895 were naturally considered by the Indian Government to be binding. Reference to the 1954 map of Chinese *irredenta*, however, shows Sikkim as a possession of the Chinese Empire 'occupied by Britain in 1889'.

(vi) Between Sikkim and the much larger (18,000 square miles) but sparsely-populated hill-state of *Bhutan*, the watershed alignment is indented by the Chumbi Valley, a wedge of Tibetan territory of considerable strategic importance. Besides providing the only direct communication between Sikkim and Bhutan from west to east, it carries from south to north the main trans-Himalayan route from Delhi to Lhasa via Yatung, with a comparatively easy pass on the Sikkim frontier (Natu La) which it is vital for India to defend. After a sequence of events similar to those in which Nepal had been concerned, Bhutan accepted British-Indian protection in a treaty of 1865, and a further treaty of 1910 left the

Bhutan Maharajah with increased financial support and complete internal authority, and the British with control of the state's foreign relations. These conditions were echoed in the treaty of friendship concluded by independent India with Bhutan on 8 August 1949. A small adjustment of the Indo-Bhutanese frontier in Bhutan's favour was made at the same time, and Bhutan undertook to prevent any export of arms and ammunition across her frontiers.

Mao Tse-tung's assumption of a claim to Bhutan as a 'lost' territory (1939) revived that of the Ch'ing Empire, whose Amban in Lhasa had written in 1904: 'The Bhutanese are the subjects of the Emperor of China who is the Lord of Heaven'—adding significantly that Bhutan was 'the gateway on the South'.

(vii) Eastwards from Bhutan, the *Indian North-East Frontier Agency* occupies some 32,000 square miles of largely tribal territory. Except for the Tawang Tract which immediately adjoins Bhutan and had in the past occasioned some minor controversies, this whole area differs in historical background from that of the frontier-states further west. The aboriginal hill-tribes lacked the minimum of state-organization necessary for diplomatic relations, nor were they seriously penetrated by Tibetan religious influence. After Assam passed into British hands with the expulsion of Burmese invaders in the First Burmese War (1826) the chief concern was to rescue the Brahmaputra plain from its long exposure to raiding from the tribal hills. In 1873 an administrative, not an international, 'Inner Line' was devised along the foot of the hills in order to control movements either way which could result in friction. The need for a definition of the boundary with Tibet along the high watershed became pressing only with the Chinese southward infiltrations that followed Chao Er-feng's violent (though short-lived) imposition of Imperial control upon Lhasa in 1910. This boundary was fixed at the Simla Conference of 1914, after the establishment of the Chinese Republic, and came to be called the McMahon Line after the British plenipotentiary. The map recording this line as the Frontier between Tibet, India and Burma (then a part of India) was accepted by the British, Tibetan and Chinese delegates. The signature of the Chinese delegate was then repudiated by the Chinese Government, *which confined its objections, however, to the boundaries as drawn between Tibet and China*. Britain subsequently signed a bipartite convention with Tibet, incorporating an identical map of the India-Tibet frontier.

Although no official Chinese objection to this frontier was ever published, Chinese maps thereafter frequently (but not invariably) placed the international frontier along the foot of the hills, where it had certainly never lain. The irredentist map of 1954 went even further, claiming as a 'lost' Chinese territory, 'given to Britain by Burma in 1826', the whole of Assam. But even before the Chinese Communist army moved into Tibet, Nehru had made clear the Indian view that the established frontier was not to be changed by such means. 'The McMahon Line,' he said on 4 May 1959, 'is our frontier, maps or no maps.' On 20 November, after the Chinese move into Tibet, he made a similar statement. And on 22 March 1951, Lhasa was officially informed of the Indian Government's intention to extend 'regular administration' right up to this international frontier.

(viii) The incorporation of *Burma* into the British-Indian Empire took place in 1886. The three Anglo-Burmese Wars of the preceding sixty years had begun as the defence of eastern India from repeated Burmese incursions. Annexation was primarily prompted by British commercial rivalry with the French, who had advanced their colonial and concessionary enterprise in Annam (Indo-China) and the southern Chinese province of Yunnan, and were competing for advantages in Upper Burma. China had not been involved in Burmese history since 1769, when the repulse of a Chinese invasion had been followed by a treaty between the King of Burma and the Manchu (Ch'ing) Emperor Ch'ien Lung on a basis of complete equality (the Mongol Empire had been similarly defeated in an attempt to conquer Lower Burma in the 14th century). Beyond the custom of a decennial exchange of presents the Chinese had no evidence for regarding Burma as a vassal, and the Burmese Supreme Council of State declared before the annexation in a Memorandum of 1 January 1886, that 'Burma has never at any time, on any account whatsoever, paid anything in the shape of tribute to China'. The British Government, however, saw advantages for future commercial relations in associating China with a settlement of Burma. The bargaining position thus offered was used by the Chinese to register opposition to British penetration in Tibet while claiming to be conceding it in Burma. This is the sole foundation for the delineation of the whole of modern Burma in Liu Pei-hua's irredentist map as a Chinese possession 'taken by the Imperialists'.

The tribal areas of Upper Burma were brought under control by 1890, and knowledge of the frontier-areas, though incomplete, was generally better on the Burmese, or British, side than on the Chinese. At Burma's northern apex the frontier with eastern Tibet—less than a hundred miles of extremely difficult country—formed the extremity of the McMahon Line boundary fixed at the Simla Conference of 1914 and not challenged, in this respect, by the Chinese. The problems of the much longer eastern frontiers with Yunnan, beyond the Irrawaddy and the Shan States, were considerably more difficult, though a watershed-boundary could be established in theory to run as far south as Bhamo, and the traditional limits of Chinese authority were—at least on a small-scale map—well enough known. A series of boundary-settlements with China was begun by the Government of India in 1897, the Chinese having then been brought to a new treaty which returned to Burma an area ceded by China to the French in contravention of the previous agreement. These boundary-discussions and surveys continued for forty years, until Burma was constitutionally detached from India in 1937. The agreement reached at this time, under a neutral League of Nations Chairman, allowed China to retain the greater part of the important mineral area in the Wa States which had been in doubt and dispute. The Japanese irruption into South-East Asia in 1941–2 prevented a final and formal settlement. But the completion of the boundary-demarcation had been agreed upon in the Sino-British notes of 18 June 1941. Recording this, the historian of modern Burma, J. L. Christian, added that 'China now has, for the first time in history, a fully delimited southern frontier from the China Sea to Turkestan'.*

FROM THE SALWEEN TO THE SEA

The eastern frontier of Burma which has just been described, together with the northern frontiers of Indo-China (Laos and North Vietnam), form a distinct zone

* In the Epilogue (completed February 1942) to his *Modern Burma*, first printed in Shanghai just before Japan's Pearl Harbour attack, reprinted in the USA with the additional chapter in 1942 (University of California Press).

in the history of China's boundaries and of her relations with her neighbours, in this case the 'countries of the southern ocean', the *Nan-Yang*. This has been a porous frontier, traditionally open to Chinese infiltration and influence, and eventually to considerable immigration. The task of Chinese dynasties had been regarded as that of ensuring political stability beyond the frontier to the advantage of trade and movement by land and sea, not that of sealing the boundary against barbarian invasion. In their advanced posts in South-East Asia the Overseas Chinese communities had acted as antennae for the first Chinese contacts with European enterprise in Asia. By the end of the 19th century, in a climate of political colonialism, they represented for Chinese nationalist writers the promise of China's revived presence in the lands of the southern ocean as a modern Power. And this preserved and even strengthened the hypothesis of Chinese superiority over the allegedly languid peoples of the south, who left so much of their development and commerce in Chinese hands.

The adoption of Communist principles of government in China, whatever its effects upon Overseas Chinese loyalties, was to face political theorists in Peking with an inescapable dilemma. For the potential instruments of Chinese influence and prestige among the *Nan-Yang* were overwhelmingly bourgeois by occupation and outlook, natural targets for revolutionary activity outside China rather than advertisements for its success inside. Only where history had provided a Chinese labour-force in industry and plantations (as in Malaya), could Chinese aggrandisement and the cause of Communism work easily in harness. And the Malayan peninsula, though falling within the claims of the less restrained irredentists, had never been a Chinese frontier-zone. The frontier-people, east of the territories of the former Burmese kings, had been for China the inhabitants of 'Annam'.

The name itself—'An-Nam', the Pacified Souht—carried suggestions of national humiliation for the population concerned. It was given to the Chinese protectorate established under the Han Empire in 111 B.C. and renewed, after numerous rebellions, by the powerful T'ang dynasty in the 7th century A.D. This took in Hanoi and the delta to the neighbourhood of the 20th parallel, in line with the Hainan Strait; but as between southern China and the protectorate the boundary was very much the line of today's international frontier. Still earlier, however, perhaps from the 3rd century B.C., a southern kingdom extended north and east of this frontier, covering a great part of the Chinese provinces of Kwangsi and Kwangtung. This was the State of Nam-Viet—'the Viet people to the South', south of China but not yet 'pacified'. Not surprisingly, it was this tradition that survived to replace the discredited name of Annam by that of Vietnam in the modern pattern of national States. So far from being pacified, it is the pride of the Viet people to have become southward colonizers in their turn, mauling or eradicating other kingdoms as they moved, during nine centuries, from the delta of the Red River to that of the Mekong. Nor is it forgotten that, despite cultural links with China and formal assumptions of its suzerainty, the Viet remained in control of their own expanding territories from the decline of T'ang power in the 10th century to the consummation of French power in the 19th. The northern frontier held. And one notable failure of the Chinese to break it is nowadays commemorated, even in a fraternal People's Republic, by a frankly publicized North

Vietnamese festival marking each anniversary of the defeat of a Manchu invasion force.

The modern acceptance of the frontiers (Laos and North Vietnam) from the Burma tri-junction to the sea began with the 1885 Treaty of Tientsin between France and China.* Frontier—conventions in 1887 and 1895 completed a detailed delimitation which has remained undisputed through subsequent political changes. The Japanese, by occupying Indo-China from 1941 to 1945, blocked China's southern supply-route across this frontier, but did not themselves advance over its 'open end' between the Red River and the sea. It was Chinese Nationalist forces that crossed it, after the defeat of Japan, under the Potsdam agreements compensating Chiang Kai-shek for Stalin's occupation-rights in Korea. This temporary Chinese control extended south to the 16th parallel, and lasted from August 1945 to February 1946, when the Chinese forces were withdrawn after agreement with the returning French. When the Chinese Communists assumed central power on 1 October 1949, France had accorded 'independance within the French Union' to Vietnam and Laos (and Cambodia). But in January 1950, Ho Chi Minh requested and received recognition of his Vietminh State from Communist China and the Soviet Union. Material military aid across the frontier, and the use of training-centres in Yunnan, were subsequently of great service to the Vietminh; and after the Korean cease-fire released quantities of Communist arms and technicians in 1953, this aid was possibly decisive.

The 265-mile section of this southern Chinese frontier that adjoins Laos has been demarcated, but it runs

---

* Not to be confused with the 1858 Treaty of Tientsin between China and Russia, cited in the *People's Daily* article of March 1963.

through rugged watershed-country where minority-peoples, not fully controlled, straddle the boundary. The same is true of the western and mountainous portion of the Sino-Vietnamese frontier. It is the last and lower course to the sea that provides the only railway-crossing, and some of the few road-crossings, in China's entire southern frontier-line of more than four thousand miles.

WARNINGS IN BURMA AND INDIA

The first country to display concern about its frontiers with the new China was the independent Union of Burma, which had also (in December 1949) been the first Asian State to recognize the Communist régime in Peking.* In Chinese Nationalist activities during and since the war against the Japanese there had been much to convince the new Burmese leaders that the Sino-British boundary accord of June 1941 had not extinguished China's territorial ambitions; and it had been found necessary to announce, in the midst of Burma's celebration of independence on 4 January 1948, that 'there is no question of Burma surrendering any piece of her territory', which would be defended against encroachment 'without any hesitation'. The KMT Government, hard-pressed as it was, had then instructed its first Ambassador in Rangoon to declare, in answer to reports of Chinese claims of 70,000 square miles, that China was prepared to negotiate 'for a final solution of the problem'. Soon after the Chinese Communist Government had replaced the Kuomintang, a Burmese approach was made to

* According to the Indian Ambassador to the Chinese CPG (the late Sardar K. M. Panikkar) India's formal recognition was delayed for a few days on a Burmese request to be allowed to be first.

Peking, suggesting a joint effort to settle and secure the frontier.

To this, however, there was no clear or helpful response. All that Mao Tse-tung's Government had to offer was an undertaking that the forces of the Chinese People's Republic would not violate Burma's borders unless they found themselves under attack from Nationalist Chinese remnants based in Burmese territory. Since the direction taken by Nationalist units in retreat from Yunnan had been across the precipitous frontier above the Salween into the very area of wild Kachin country which had been the subject of Chinese claims, the Communist attitude was anything but reassuring. The sequence was predictable. Chinese Communist units were apparently intruding in the Triangle area, north of Myitkyina, by 1951. Next year they were reported in the Kawa area, ostensibly in pursuit of Nationalist troops. In reply to Burmese protests Peking admitted the location of its forces but disputed that it was Burmese territory. After further incursions in January 1953, this time of Yunnan-trained guerillas into the Shan and Kachin States,* the Burma Government made renewed but unsuccessful attempts to draw the Chinese People's Government into frontier-negotiations.

A further source of Burmese uneasiness was found in the apparent claims of Chinese maps— 'cartographical aggression', as it came to be loosely called. Under the Kuomintang the maps published in China had frequently included as Chinese territory some 10,000 square miles of northern Burma (as seen in international atlases) down

---

* It was later confirmed that these operations had aims other than the liquidation of remnant Chinese Nationalists. In April 1955, when Chou En-lai was in Rangoon on his way home from Bandung, he admitted (as revealed by U Nu) having granted asylum in Yunnan to the Kachin rebel Naw Seng and two hundred of his followers.

to the region of Myitkina. In December 1950, a map issued under the Communist régime carried the frontier (though shown as 'undemarcated') still further south to Bhamo. Early next year a map taking in a large part of the Kachin States appeared in publications openly displayed by the Chinese Embassy in Rangoon. The official Peking explanation, in reply to representations, was conveyed to Parliament by the Burmese Premier U Nu on 9 March 1951: 'The Chinese Government had no time to draw up a new map and had reproduced the old one.' The matter had not been rectified two years later, when a map officially released by Peking for wide circulation showed the Irrawaddy flowing through South-West China.

The same map also led to complaints from India, in respect of its apparent annexations of Indian territory. On this and many subsequent occasions the Chinese explanation was in the same terms as that offered to Burma— a plea that the Communist Government had been too preoccupied to rectify the cartographical assumptions of its predecessors.

Inaccurate maps are published, of course, in most countries from time to time. But there were plausible reasons for the effect which the Chinese attitude to this question came at length to exert upon both public and official opinion in India. Chinese evasiveness could hardly appear less than deliberate when set beside the care taken by the Indian Government to define from the beginning its acceptance of a northern frontier inherited by the transfer of British authority, and to establish its own treaty-relationships with the frontier-States. The treaty with Bhutan, as has already been noted, was concluded in August 1949, before the collapse of the Kuomintang in China. The treaty with independent Nepal dated from

31 January 1950, after the establishment of the Chinese People's Government but before it had moved forces into Tibet. The treaty with Sikkim followed in December 1950. It was before the Chinese advance into Tibet, moreover, that Nehru had clarified Indian policy by stating in Parliament that Indian security would immediately be affected by any violation of Nepal's northern frontier.

As to the McMahon Line sector, there is evidence that in October 1950 the Chinese themselves were not disposed to dispute the Indian position. Chinese units moving into Tibet 'to defend China's frontiers' were reported to have strayed over the Indian border in its eastern extremities, but they were persuaded without difficulty to withdraw. It would have seemed that Nehru's clear public statement on behalf of India that 'the McMahon Line is our boundary', made as early as 20 November 1950, could not possibly be ignored by a neighbouring Power believing, if it did so believe, that it had a valid title to some 40,000 square miles of territory south of that line. Even after several repetitions, however, the Chinese Government ignored it. The announcement that they regarded the entire frontier with India and its protected Hill-States as undefined and subject to fresh negotiation was not made until 1959, when it emerged as a consequence of their political failure in Tibet and their political mistrust of India.

On the Sino-Burmese frontier, where menacing Chinese maps and evasive Chinese assurances had sown much the same seeds, a major dispute was to be avoided only by a pragmatic Chinese decision that in this case a frontier-settlement was worth obtaining, even at the cost of compromise.

THE BANDUNG PHASE: 1954-9

FRONTIERS AND THE FIVE PRINCIPLES

It was after the Asian-African Conference at Bandung, in Indonesia, in April 1955, that the words *Panch Shila* (sometimes, in India, *Panchasheel*) became widely used in Asian politics. The 'Five Principles' to which they referred, however, had first been mentioned just a year earlier, when they were embodied in the Sino-Indian Agreement on Trade and Intercourse between the Tibet Region of China and India, concluded on 29 April 1954. And in August of the same year they had been accepted, in joint statements made by Chou En-lai with Nehru in Delhi and with Nu in Rangoon, as governing relations between China and India and between China and Burma.

Although it might be said that the Five Principles in themselves did little more than describe a state of international relations normal in time of peace, their formulation was widely interpreted as opening a new phase and marking a new kind of accord. Even after the USSR had been brought into the pattern in the Nehru-Bulganin joint announcement of June 1955, a specially Asian quality was attributed to the initiative.

The first two Principles ('peaceful coexistence' was No. 5) had some bearing on frontier-questions. They were:

(1) Mutual respect for each other's territorial integrity and sovereignty.

(2) Mutual non-aggression.

When the Sino-Indian Agreement on Tibet had run its initial eight-year course, an Indian note to the Chinese Government (11 April 1962) said pertinently:

> The Agreement of 1954 was obviously intended to settle all outstanding issues which had been inherited from the past. . . . The Chinese side had full knowledge at the time of what constituted the territorial boundaries of India. If it had any doubt, what was the purpose of the undertaking which it gave to respect India's territorial integrity?

But those words were written when the outward cordiality of the 1954 Agreement had vanished in a deepening dispute. The Agreement was originally regarded by the Indian Government as having saved what could be saved of the Indian position in Tibet, relinquished what was untenable, and established the possibility of resolving Sino-Indian questions by discussion.

For the Chinese the 1954 negotiations secured a principle of great importance from their viewpoint, and one which was to affect the whole aspect of subsequent frontier-argument. The description of Tibet as a 'Region of China' acknowledged the conversion of its long southern boundary with India into a Chinese boundary. As to where that boundary lay, however, no question was raised in the discussions preceding the Agreement. Since the matters to be resolved were stated to be those of trade and intercourse across the frontier, this was of peculiar significance.

It had been at China's suggestion that questions relating to frontiers were excluded in advance, and to this the Indian negotiators had agreed. It may have occurred to both sides that the problem 'left over by history' of India's relations with Tibet should properly be taken up at the point where it had been left at Simla in 1914, in the

Conventions agreed directly between the Tibetan and Indian authorities. It was in China's interest to ignore these altogether. Where they had related to trade-arrangements and Indian establishments in Tibet they could be patently superseded by negotiating new terms of relationship. A boundary, however, could not so easily be rendered null and void; and to define a fresh one, even if it were to be along the same alignment, would involve appeals to the authority of the existing one. This was indeed to present obvious difficulties to the Chinese more than six years later, when they were brought to submit their frontier-claims to examination. In 1954 the better part of diplomacy was to keep frontier-matters out of the discussions. As for India, agreement to this proposal not only improved the prospects for a reasonably rapid settlement of other difficulties. It appeared to rule out, if only tacitly, any subsequent Chinese move towards frontier-changes.

That appearance was deceptive. Undoubtedly the text of the 1954 Agreement favoured the assumption of a frontier jointly accepted and understood. It dealt with routes and conditions of entry, provided for the examination of documents at checkpoints, and specified six Himalayan passes to be used by 'traders and pilgrims of both countries'. But an ominous note, unrecorded in the text, had entered the talks when the Chinese proposed to phrase these arrangements as a Chinese act of opening passes lying wholly within Chinese territory. Bearing in mind that a pass can be twenty or thirty miles long, covering the ascent from a grazing or camping-ground in one country and the descent to the first sign of occupation in another, the Indians adhered to the usual concept of a boundary located at the highest point. They won the argument, but not without difficulty, the Chinese record-ing that 'this was the sixth concession made by the Chinese side'.

Within three months of the signing of the Agreement on Trade and Intercourse the supposed tranquillity of the frontier had been interrupted by the first of a long series of incidents. The small area concerned, near the Niti Pass which was among those named as routes of entry into Tibet, was commonly referred to as Wu-Je by the Chinese (who made the initial complaint) and as Hoti or Barahoti by the Indians, who alleged a Chinese intrusion. Seasonal movement to grazing-grounds had in the past produced occasions of jurisdictional uncertainty in this locality, but there was no inherent reason for a major dispute. Con-fusion of names and the limited Chinese knowledge of local geography were enough to start the argument; but in the course of it the Chinese reinforced the hint they had already given by arguing their right to extend the control of a pass down to its southern approaches.

The Indian Government, for its part, gave early notice of what it expected of the Five Principles by complaining (27 August 1954) that Chinese action at this point was not in conformity with the recently signed Agreement on Tibet, nor with the 'spirit of the joint communiqué' even more recently issued over the names of the two Prime Ministers. Premier Nu of Burma, armed with a similar joint declaration of *Panch Shila*, returned Chou En-lai's visit to Rangoon by going to Peking at the end of 1954. In the atmosphere of Asian amiability, writes one autho-rity, 'any subject as specific as a boundary question seemed almost an indecent interruption'.* But U Nu did, by his own later account, take occasion to point out that Burma,

* Dorothy Woodman: *The Making of Modern Burma* (1962).

though powerless to endanger China by herself, was well placed to make herself a nuisance by offering 'key locations' and facilities to a potential opponent. He achieved no firm Chinese undertaking to negotiate a frontier-settlement, and the joint communiqué of 12 December 1954, vague as it was, left a lever of 'incomplete delimitation' in Chinese hands: 'In view of the incomplete delimitation of the boundary-line between China and Burma, the two Premiers held it necessary to settle this question in a friendly spirit at an appropriate time through normal diplomatic channels.'

BANDUNG AND ITS AFTERMATH

Four months later, at the Bandung Conference of twenty-nine Asian and African States, Chou En-lai pointed to China's adoption of the Five Principles* in her relations with India and Burma as having been undertaken 'to alleviate doubts which many countries have of China'. On the first Principle, concerning respect for territorial integrity, the Chinese Premier remarked that 'we have common borders with four countries'. Without explaining which were the unacknowledged States among China's ten neighbours (twelve if Sikkim and Bhutan are included, fourteen with the addition of Hongkong and Macao) he went on:

  With some of these countries we have not yet finally fixed our border-line and we are ready to do so with our neighbouring countries. But before doing so, we are willing to maintain the present situation by acknowledging that those parts of our border are parts which are undetermined. We are ready to restrain our Government and people from crossing even one step across our border.

  * There was an increase of points of principle at this time, first to 7, and in the final Bandung communiqué of 24 April 1955 to 10. But it was the original Five Principles which gained common usage.

If such things should happen, we would like to admit our mistake. As to the determination of common borders which we are going to undertake with our neighbouring countries, we shall use only peaceful means and we shall not permit any other kinds of method. In no case shall we change this.

Assurances of a disposition to use peaceful means in the question of Taiwan, and to negotiate with Indonesia regarding the status of its Overseas Chinese population, were among Chou En-lai's conciliatory gestures during the Bandung Conference. The only border-problem specifically cited was that with Burma, and here Chou used the presence of Chinese Nationalist remnant forces to turn criticism of subversive Communist tactics in a different direction:

The problem at present is not that we are carrying out subversive activities against the Governments of other countries, but that there are people who are establishing bases around China in order to carry out subversive activities against the Chinese Government. For instance, on the border between China and Burma, there are in fact remnant armed elements of the Chiang Kai-shek clique who are carrying out destructive activities against both China and Burma.

In the light of the problem thus stated, if for no other reason, the 'appropriate time' for proceeding to a settlement of the Sino-Burmese border might be thought to have arrived. But five and a half years and much hard bargaining were to pass before a boundary treaty reached signature in Peking (1 October 1960). Some of the delay could be attributed to changes in the Burma Government, and in particular to the political crisis of 1958. But in 1955 the first sequel to the Bandung declaration of Asian concord had been the increased movement of Chinese Communist troops into Burma. In November of that year a serious clash occurred when they met Burmese units engaged on a flag march in the Wa States, on the western or Burma side of the boundary accepted by the Chinese Nationalist Government in 1941. Remonstrances from Rangoon caused Peking to challenge the 1941 line as having been imposed by the British on a Chinese administration weakened by Japan's aggression. The theme was familiar, but it ignored the circumstance of Britain's own critical situation in 1941. In fact *both* parties to the unfinalized agreement of 1941 had felt the Japanese threat as compulsive, and China had come off with some advantage.

The Wa incident showed a pattern which was to be repeated again and again in the case of Chinese frontier-conflict with India. Peking proposed that '*pending the settlement of the entire boundary through negotiation, both sides should maintain the status quo*'—thus foreshadowing the tactics of establishing a 'line of actual control' by military action as a bargaining-counter in eventual discussions. Resisting this, the Burmese suggested the avoidance of further clashes by the withdrawal of both sides to an agreed distance on either side of the 1941 line, after which a joint boundary-commission should examine the question of the boundary in the section where it was undelimited. This the Chinese rejected, as they were to reject proposals on the same lines put forward by India.

It was Burmese policy, and Indian policy also, to give no publicity to frontier-disputes and exchanges with the Chinese, so as not to jeopardize good relations and the hopes of a secure frontier. In Burma the problem was forced into the open as early as August 1956, when the Rangoon *Nation* published a sensational account of the Chinese intrusions. In the circumstances the report could not be accurate, but it drew an admission from the

Burmese Government that some 500 Chinese troops were on Burmese territory, over an area of 700–1,000 square miles. In India official reticence was broadly effective until the dramatic developments in Tibet in 1959, ard the first Indian release of documents was made only in September of that year. Nevertheless the post-Bandung atmosphere of fervent but artificial Sino-Indian friendship was contaminated from time to time by journalistic speculations on the frontier-situation and by serious enquiries in Parliament, although the fact that the main Opposition was provided by the Communist Party helped to keep criticism of Peking to a minimum. At the same time the Chinese explanation of their disturbing maps was bound to appear progressively less plausible. Within a week or two of the final Bandung communiqué, Indian trade-unionists invited to Peking for the May Day celebrations curtailed their visit in protest against the public display in the Chinese capital of a map showing Kashmir as a Chinese possession.

In the Middle Sector of the Indian Frontier the well-known and well-marked pass of Shipki La was the scene of a Chinese intrusion on 8 September 1956. Though the Indian Government insisted that any crossing of this border pass would be considered as aggression and resisted, its local Security Force was instructed not to take action for the present. Later the Chinese were to claim the Shipki Pass among localities which 'definitely belonged to China'. Further incidents prolonged the argument over Wu-Je and Hoti, where the Chinese professed themselves open to a negotiated settlement but resisted Indian moves to neutralize the area during discussion. Not until April 1958 was it possible to bring this localized problem to a conference-table in Delhi. China's official delegates declined to move from their opposition to the Indian proposal that during these negotiations neither side should attempt to exercise control, military or civil, of the area in question. The argument, therefore, remained where it was, though it proved of relatively small importance beside the large territories that were presently to be brought into dispute.

To bring them into dispute was the object of Chinese policy, not to settle an already existing conflict. It is at this stage that both the similarities and the differences in Communist China's frontier-relations with India and Burma begin to be seen. In the case of Burma a largely delimited frontier was held to rest upon rejected history, upon agreements accepted under duress by a former, and weaker, Chinese Government. In the case of India the Chinese were to suggest, yet more speciously, that the frontier had 'never been formally delimited'.* The main impulsion to take up this position arose from the circumstance that the greater part of India's northern frontier lay with Tibet, whose past competence to treat with foreign Governments it was essential to obscure.

But however the two situations might be viewed in Peking, there is no evidence that frontier-stabilization was desired as a matter of urgency, or even of priority. Progress in the Sino-Burmese negotiations, slow as it was, was maintained only by Burmese insistence that satisfactory political relations depended upon a settlement. The Chinese view, it is reasonably clear, was contrary: that a settlement depended upon friendly relations. And these, it could be assumed from several public statements, required at least a measure of ideological support for China's

---

* 'Delimitation' and 'demarcation' are frequently confused or equated in Chinese statements on frontier-questions.

international policies. With broader issues at stake, a fluid and uncertain frontier-situation was by no means inconvenient for the Chinese, who by tradition have not been inclined to confine their influence within rigid cartographical limits. The final solution of a frontier-question by treaty would obviously eliminate it as a counter in the larger commerce of politics, whether Chinese or Communist. It might thus be expected that only the prospect of some compensating political gain would bring Peking to recognize the 'appropriate time' for a settlement. This in fact is the pattern which Chinese frontier-tactics were to follow.

On the other side of the boundaries, Burmese and Indian approaches to the subject naturally differed from each other. Burma had the old experience of an outmoded relationship which China assumed to be one of vassalage, and the new experience of Chinese military incursions and border subversions among the first problems of Burmese independence. These were good enough reasons to press for a frontier-treaty. Neither of them applied to the new India, whose Government had every incentive to assume and clearly assert that its inherited frontiers were valid, and to build a policy of amicable relations with China on that foundation. The onus of raising a frontier-question, if they had one to raise, was thus left to the Chinese. They did not raise one by allowing vaguely expansionist maps to appear. But these, with the evasiveness of Peking's explanations of the matter, did indicate a desire to keep open the possibility of a dispute, and to diminish the ultimate force of the Indian assumption. The Chinese did not find the 1954 negotiations—on a relevant issue and at a time of comparative harmony—to be an appropriate occasion for declaring, and solving, a frontier-question.

But although these tactics offered rational support to the Indian standpoint, the agreement on Tibet had other consequences. By converting India's former status in Tibet to a new relationship (and one which the Chinese, as was shortly seen, could infringe in practice), the agreement reduced the bargaining factors available to India on any future occasion of difference. And by confirming China's freedom to activate the frontier-zone in a military sense, it increased the probability of local altercations, whether they arose accidentally or in consequence of deliberate probing. Sooner or later what India regarded as unquestionable would prove to be in question.

The first of such local incidents, as we have noticed, followed within a few weeks of the signing of the agreement on Tibet. As others occurred, the confidential notes exchanged between the two Governments seemed to indicate that both were reluctant to impair the good-will officially subsisting between them. The framing of their communications, however, showed significant differences. To the Indian Government violations of their understood frontiers amounted to violations of the *Panch Shila* and carried a threat to friendly relations. Chinese counterallegations, on the other hand, even at their most peremptory, maintained the idea that border-clashes and disagreements were secondary and transient matters, irrelevant to a long-term political relationship which must eventually dissolve them. China and India, this attitude seemed to suggest, could live with a general frontier-problem— but India must be brought to appreciate that there was one.

INDIA, BURMA AND THE MCMAHON LINE

Apart from the cases of apologetic trespass during the Chinese move into eastern Tibet in 1950, the first incident

93

reported from India's North-East Frontier Agency occurred in October 1957 in the extreme corner near the India-Burma-Tibet trijunction. A year later a larger Chinese military party, according to Indian information, camped on the Indian side and then crossed over into Burmese territory. The security of the Talok-Diphu Pass between

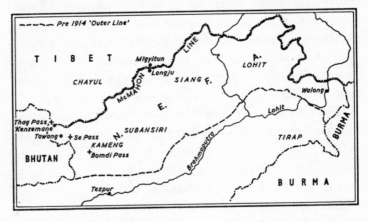

5. Sino-Indian Frontier: Eastern Sector

India (Assam) and Burma had been an item of some importance in Sir Henry McMahon's line as agreed with Tibet at Simla in 1914, and detailed topographical material had been obtained for the area of the trijunction and the watershed alignment of Burma's northern boundary. The course of Burma's efforts to confirm her frontiers with China was of natural interest to India, and more particularly at this point. And in 1956 Nu privately asked Nehru if he could exert any influence in Peking on Burma's behalf. The Indian Prime Minister, according to the account of the matter which he gave five years later in the Upper House, framed a tactful message to Chou En-lai, suggesting that he might invite Nu (who by then was no longer Prime Minister of Burma) for talks on the subject. One line of persuasion that Nehru used he remembered particularly:

I said Burma is relatively a small country; on the either side of Burma are these big countries China and India, and Burma naturally feels a little apprehensive of both these countries . . . and it is up to us to function in a way to remove all apprehension from the mind of Burma which is a friendly country.

The Chinese invitation was despatched, but not on Nehru's recommendation alone. On visits to Peking the Prime Minister of Pakistan and President Sukarno of Indonesia had added to the weight of Asian concern that *Panch Shila* pretensions should be shown to have some effect in a frontier-question between Asian countries. U Nu had his Peking talks, and on 9 November 1956 the *People's Daily* dealt with his friendly visit in connection with a problem 'left over by history'. The paper concluded that 'the most favourable conditions exist for a settlement of the boundary question'. It was a general settlement that Nu had sought to promote, and on his return to Rangoon he informed the Press that 'China has agreed to recognize the McMahon Line in the interests of an overall settlement of frontiers between Burma and China'.

Chou En-lai had perhaps preferred to deal at this point with U Nu, who was not only amiable but out of office, rather than with the more stubborn Prime Minister U Ba Swe. But Nu had had a full mission with him, including Kachin representatives; and the latter had declined to commit their people finally to the cession of three Kachin villages which (though they had never been Chinese) had been the scene of a clash with the British and were now required by the Chinese Communists as a face-saving item. Nor had Chou, of course, referred directly to the McMahon Line, which in itself had to be reserved as an 'imperialist' imposition. What he had done was to agree in principle to the alignment of Burma's northern and north-eastern boundary—with the exception of the three coveted villages—along a watershed system which included the easternmost sector of the McMahon Line. Next month Chou was himself in Rangoon, returning Nu's visit and finding much popular, as well as official, objection to the cession of the Kachin villages. His talks with U Ba Swe achieved no more than a 'further clarification of the Chinese and Burmese points of view' and a reaffirmation of the Five Principles.

From Rangoon Chou went to Delhi, and in the course of confidential talks with Nehru referred to the present state of the Sino-Burmese frontier-discussions on which the Indian Prime Minister had already been briefed by U Nu. An informal minute taken by Nehru during the conversations ran as follows:

Premier Chou referred to the McMahon Line and again said that he had never heard of this before though of course the then Chinese Government had dealt with this matter and not accepted that line. He had gone into this matter in connection with the border dispute with Burma. Although he thought that this line, established by British Imperialists, was not fair, nevertheless, because it was an accomplished fact and because of the friendly relations which existed between China and the countries concerned, namely India and Burma, the Chinese Government was of the opinion that they should give recognition to the McMahon Line. They had, however, not consulted the Tibetan authorities about it yet. They proposed to do so.

The Chinese assurance represented in this record, and its progressive whittling down until India's occupancy of her entire North-East Frontier Agency came to be denounced by China as illegal aggression, became of crucial importance in the subsequent relations of the two countries. The Indian Prime Minister's sense of personal betrayal was enlarged, when the matter became public property in September 1959, into a national resentment which in itself would have rendered a compromise solution of the frontier-dispute impossible within a parliamentary democracy. And the impression of Chinese perfidy was deepened when it became clear that China had finally settled her boundary with northern Burma on a principle which she refused to apply to her boundary with India.

It is open to doubt, however, that Chou En-lai regarded himself as giving any assurance of this kind in his conversations with Nehru. And the first thing that should be remembered is that, strictly speaking, Nehru did not require one. The basis of the Indian frontier from Bhutan to the trijunction was secured by international agreement, had been repeatedly reaffirmed, and had not been openly challenged. To discuss Chinese acceptance of it at all was to open it to possible dispute. And this, as has already been suggested, was precisely what Chinese political tactics required. It is therefore important to notice that, according to Nehru's testimony in a subsequent letter to Chou En-lai,* it was the latter who introduced the Sino-Burmese border into the conversation, and in this connection mentioned 'the Sino-Indian border, and more especially the so-called McMahon Line'. Having thus succeeded in raising the subject he brought it into argument, as the record shows, with some interesting Chinese contentions:

(i) The establishment of the frontier-line by 'British Imperialists' rendered it questionable.

* 14 December 1958. It was the release of this letter in the First Indian White Paper, 7 September 1959, which first gave publicity to Nehru's minute on the point at issue.

(ii) The Chinese Government was in a position to give or with-hold recognition of this frontier as it might decide.

(iii) If recognition were given it would be a concession (a) to an 'accomplished fact' rather than an existing legality, thus leaving the Chinese some liberty to produce a different 'accomplished fact'; and (b) to a state of 'friendly relations' of which China could call for particular proofs from India.

(iv) Nothing more could be expected of the Chinese Government until they had 'consulted the Tibetan authorities'.

This last point was curious, since the Chinese Government had not only taken over in 1951 the 'centralized handling of all external affairs of the area of Tibet', but also repudiated any past Tibetan competence to conclude frontier-agreements with foreign Powers. It seems probable that the Chinese Prime Minister was preparing the way for a Chinese use of earlier Tibetan claims of monastic jurisdiction south of the Indian border. He may also have been drawing oblique attention to the part that Tibet's internal situation might play in future Chinese frontier-policy. During 1956 the Kham revolt had attained serious proportions, and it had been impossible to prevent reports of battle and massacre from reaching India and the outside world. Both the Dalai Lama and the Panchen Lama, with numerous advisers, were at that moment in India for the Buddhist 2,500th anniversary— so that in fact Chou En-lai could have 'consulted the Tibetan authorities' then and there. His chief concern, however, was to convince Nehru that Chinese Communist rule in Tibet was both benign and indestructible, and to enlist his aid in overcoming the Dalai Lama's private doubts about returning to Lhasa.

If the absence of any forward movement along the McMahon Line frontier during the next two years seemed to reinforce what Nehru had accepted as a Chinese assurance, a map published in the *China Pictorial* in July 1958 served the more genuine Chinese purpose of keeping the question open. The magazine was an official, multilingual organ of Chinese foreign publicity, circulated in India in the mutual freedom of cultural relations. The Chinese People's Government had now had more than nine years in which to consider where their frontiers lay. The map nevertheless enclosed as Chinese, a large though un-detailed area south of the McMahon Line, and another in Ladakh in the west.

In Burma, where the Premiership which U Nu had resumed was once more slipping from his hands, the frontier-talks had made little progress, despite Chou En-lai's report to the National People's Congress a year earlier (9 July 1957) that the two Governments had 'arrived at a general agreement of views on the boundary question'. One difficulty that had arisen in the confidential official exchanges was Chou En-lai's retreat from the watershed principle, where he was insisting on preliminary joint surveys before committing himself, at the same time introducing new points concerning monastic and other titles to properties south of the watershed. This appeared to the Burmese to reopen a prospect of considerable Chinese claims and endless argument, and they deter-mined to press (as General Ne Win was in the end to press successfully), for an unconditional acceptance of the water-shed.

Another difficulty confronted the question of exchang-ing territories of double claim, in this case the three Kachin villages on the one hand and the Namwan Assigned Tract (under an existing lease agreement) on the other. 'Both these areas,' Chou En-lai contended, 'legally belonged to China, and it was therefore not possible for one to be exchanged for the other.' This was an argument of potential significance to the question of China's frontiers with India, in which the Chinese edged their dispute in the direction of territorial exchanges only to make them virtually unnegotiable.

LADAKH AND THE AKSAI CHIN

The key area of Sino-Indian conflict in the lofty and virtually uninhabited wilderness of north-eastern Ladakh did not come within the scope of serious representations before the summer of 1958. It had, of course, figured in the major cartographical discrepancies to which Chinese attention had been drawn on different occasions, and the Indian Government's understanding of its historic boundaries in that region had been indicated in the general maps published in 1950, 1954 and 1956. The complex topography in which the Tibetan plateau met the Kun Lun and Karakoram ranges did not rule out an appeal to natural principles in boundary-fixing; but it provided nothing so simple in its essentials as the watershed-line of the Assam Himalaya in the east. Nor did the political boundaries, which were those of the former principality of Kashmir with Tibet on the east and Sinkiang on the north, offer a single treaty-basis, like that of the Mc-Mahon Line, for designating the frontier which India proposed to maintain.

The nearest approach to a 'McMahon Line' for Ladakh was something which never came into effect—the Mac-Donald Alignment (or Macartney-MacDonald Alignment) of 1899. In the subsequent course of the Sino-Indian dispute the note communicated by Sir Claude MacDonald, the British Minister, to the Foreign Ministry at Peking on 14 March 1899, was quoted differently

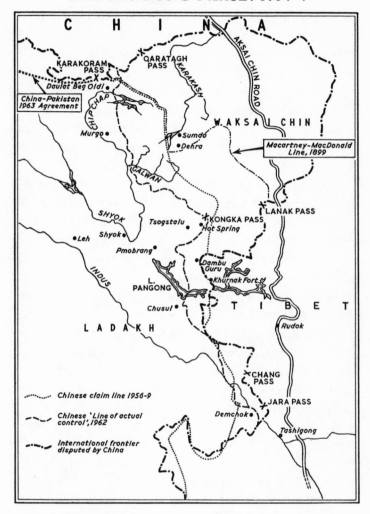

6. Sino-Indian Frontier: Western Sector

and in different senses by Indian and Chinese spokesmen, and it is still a matter of controversy among foreign specialists. What can be said is that this note represented a serious attempt to describe a boundary on the north and north-east of Ladakh in terms of natural features; that it embodied a deliberate concession of territory to the Chinese Empire; and that this proposed concession covered the whole of the course to be taken half a century later by the road which the Chinese Communists considered to be strategically vital. But what is at least equally important is that the offer produced no reply, nor even an acknowledgment, from Peking, and thus became void.

The MacDonald proposal had in fact been attached as an inducement in a final attempt to associate China with an international settlement at the western end of the Karakoram, at the junction of empires in the High Pamir. The Chinese, having already declined to take part in the establishment of agreed boundaries at this point between the British Empire, the Russian Empire and Afghanistan, affected to consider that settlement as a 'secret treaty' and were not interested in securing it by formally recognizing the extension of the boundary which affected Hunza— even though this would have assisted their own claim to a suzerain interest in Hunza at one end of the Karakoram, and at the other would have revised the maps of the Aksai Chin to their advantage.

Behind the Communist approach to the problems of this area there was thus the disinclination of the later Manchu Empire to enter into any conclusive delimitation of frontiers. And so little was the Chinese Communist Government concerned with exact or legalized definitions in this little-known border-zone that, when their dispute with India required them to make a case for international consumption, they converted the ignored offer of 1899 into a British *annexation* of the Aksai Chin. Even the official maps produced under the Chinese People's Republic showed a bewildering difference of alignment in this area when they later came to be offered for Indian inspection. Not only was it difficult to be sure of the real extent of their claims, but they finally introduced, as authority, two large-scale maps which had never been published. These were secret military maps made in 1918 for the Chinese General Staff and in 1943 for the Ministry of Defence. As such, they could not be accepted as internationally authoritative. What they did prove was that Chinese interest in the Aksai Chin had for long been a strategic one.

In pursuing it the Chinese Communists had shown indifference to other aspects of the matter rather than ignorance of them. If it had occurred to them, either before the 1954 affirmation of a *Panch Shila* relationship or in the years immediately following it, to discuss with a friendly India a frontier-accord in this desolate area which would safeguard China's necessary communications, the idea had been put aside without trial. It seemed more satisfactory, when the road-system and its military outposts should come to be discovered, to be able to point out that the unmade route over the Aksai Chin had been used in 1950-1 in the operations to secure Tibet, that surveying for the Sinkiang–Tibet highway had taken place between 1954 and 1955, and that a motorable road had been constructed with a large local labour-force, between March 1956 and October 1957. Possession, in other words, would be nine points of the law, and an Indian assertion of her rights in 'custom and administration' would be difficult to substantiate.

The first indication of Indian concern in this sector, given on 2 July 1958, referred to a brief Chinese intrusion at Khurnak in the Pangong Lake area, in the extreme south of the Ladakh-Tibet border—a trivial affair until it fell into a pattern of Chinese claims extending far beyond the high plateau and its crossing. Indian knowledge of the Chinese road itself (at all events at its northern entry into Ladakh from Sinkiang at Haji Langar and its south-eastern exit, with several motorable branches, near the Amtogar Lake) was communicated a few months afterwards in a protest of 18 October. In this case the Chinese were notified of the disappearance of an Indian patrol, for which they later admitted responsibility and returned the captured party.

Already in these first exchanges the Indian Government supplied memoranda of the evidence, in treaties and other documents, on which it based its understanding of the boundaries of Ladakh. The Chinese offered neither a refutation of the Indian assumptions nor a basis for their own, which reinforces the impression that they had not up to this point considered the legalities of the question. They did, however, draw from the Indian Government, on 8 November 1958, an admission that 'the question whether the particular area (traversed by the Chinese road) is in Indian or Chinese territory is a matter of dispute which has to be dealt with separately'.

This is of some importance. The Indian complaint of three weeks earlier had regretted that the Chinese Government 'should have constructed a road *through indisputably Indian territory* without first obtaining the permission of the Government of India and without even informing the Government of India'. Since it now appeared that the Chinese claimed the area, the Indian Government proposed to prepare a detailed statement of its own argument. Here, therefore, in a section of the Sino-Indian frontier of great concern to the Chinese, Nehru and his Government recognized a matter that was open to negotiation and possible adjustment. Despite the conviction that they had been treated with a good deal less than the frankness to be expected between *Panch Shila* associates, they continued to keep this possibility open until other factors in a deepening conflict induced them to harden their position. Even in the highly charged situation of September 1959, the Indian Prime Minister made it clear in a parliamentary debate that the region traversed by the Chinese road fell in a different category from that of the McMahon Line: 'This place—Aksai Chin area—is in our maps undoubtedly, but I distinguish it completely from other areas. It is a matter for argument as to what part of it belongs to us and what part of it belongs to someone else — it is not at all a dead clear matter. . . . That particular area stands by itself.'

One reason for the failure to localize and settle the dispute before it had been opened to nation-wide debate in India was certainly the Chinese reluctance to define their claims. In other parts of the frontier this vagueness bore several interpretations. In the Aksai Chin region it can be inferred that the strategic requirements of their position in Sinkiang were not fixed, but fluid. While the Indian approach took into account a degree of weakness or uncertainty in its juridical position in this sector of the frontier, the Chinese gave no indication of having examined the strength of their own claim. They were not so much defending an old frontier as looking for a new one that would meet their existing, and anticipated, security needs. Within limits they could have negotiated for Indian compliance. But if the limits were in any serious doubt, India's own security would become a factor in the argument. The Cease-Fire Line with Pakistan in Kashmir ended theoretically at the Karakoram Pass, only some fifty miles west of the point at which the Chinese road entered Ladakh from Sinkiang. Any Chinese tendency to widen the coveted area on the flank of the road would before long threaten the Indian defence-corridor through Leh, quite apart from the implications of a Chinese Communist advance towards the inhabited region of Buddhist Ladakh.

It was for this reason that Chinese cartographical claims in this area continued to concern the Indian Government. The *China Pictorial* map of July 1958, which has already been mentioned in connection with the McMahon Line, also marked the greater part of Ladakh as falling within China. An official Indian suggestion that the corrections for which the Chinese Government had not previously found time should be delayed no longer, had met with no reply when the issue of the Aksai Chin road was broached in October. When an answer was given on 3 November it was, to say the least, evasive:

The Chinese Government believes that with the elapse of time, and after consultations with the various neighbouring countries and a survey of the border regions, a new way of drawing the boundary of China will be decided on in accordance with the results of the consultation and the survey.

THE ROOTS OF DISPUTE

At the end of 1958, nine years after the establishment of the Chinese People's Government, the position on its 2,000-mile frontier with India was thus as follows:

(1) Two relatively small but significant areas of dispute had been identified. One was a lofty plain, with a village and a camping-ground, south of the Niti Pass in the Garwhal Himalaya. The other, larger in extent but hitherto

humanly unimportant, was the extreme north-eastern corner of Ladakh where the Chinese had found the only feasible alignment for their Sinkiang–Tibet road-link. The first question had been brought to the conference table in Delhi, where talks had broken down because the Chinese would only negotiate from a position of 'actual control' of the disputed area. On the second question the Indian Government had stated its intention to produce a detailed case. In the meantime both areas remained in Chinese physical occupation.

(2) Over the greater part of the frontier the Sino-Indian Agreement on Trade and Intercourse with Tibet had bilaterally recognized Tibet's southern boundaries as a Chinese responsibility. It had at the same time allowed it to be assumed that no general difference of opinion on the location of the frontier existed, or was likely to arise between friendly countries pledged to respect each other's territorial integrity. The Chinese militarization of this frontier, however, had led to intrusions at several widely-scattered points and could be expected to produce more.

(3) On long and specific sectors of the frontier the Indian Government had made clear its policy of regarding Nepal's northern boundary as inviolable, of adhering to Indian treaty-responsibilities in respect of Sikkim and Bhutan, and of maintaining the McMahon Line boundary east of Bhutan to the trijunction with Burma.

(4) None of these Indian positions had as yet been officially challenged by China, and the Indian Prime Minister had been privately informed by the Chinese Prime Minister of his Government's intention to recognize the boundary represented by the McMahon Line. Nevertheless, the publication of Chinese maps taking in territory south of the McMahon Line and in the Ladakh

salient, to a total of roughly 50,000 square miles, had persisted in the face of repeated Indian representations.

The circulation of these maps had, in fact, reached a point where it could only be held to be fully calculated. In these circumstances Nehru initiated the personal correspondence with Chou En-lai which thereafter—at intervals — was to form an important channel for the expression of the two countries' views and positions. The first three letters that passed between them (14 December 1958– 22 March 1959), though comparatively short and carefully cordial, laid bare the roots of a great deal of subsequent argument.

As the question came to force itself upon world attention, an increasing place in the argument was naturally taken by the problems of a peaceful settlement and the conflicting claims of both sides to be seeking it. It is therefore important to recognize, as the controversy shaped itself at the turn of 1958–9, that neither side—though for different reasons—gave evidence of desiring a settlement at all. The Indians believed that a frontier already existed, obviously strong in its general natural justification, and historically supported either by treaties or by traditional usage or by both. That much of it was not demarcated (marked on the ground) was reasonably attributed to the formidable nature of the terrain and the connected factor of a largely undisturbed history. It did not require a 'peaceful settlement'. It simply required, in its general configuration, to be respected. This at no time excluded the possibility of negotiating local adjustments as and where either country had a point of difference to raise.

At Barahoti and in the Aksai Chin the Indian Government had recognized such points of difference. In his opening letter Nehru played down the former as a petty matter (though hoping for an agreed outcome) and did not mention the latter. This undoubtedly reflected the great weight he attached to maintaining the validity of the frontier as a whole under the increasing menace of the Chinese manipulation of their extensive map-claims. 'There can be no question of these large parts of India being anything but India and there is no dispute about them.' The Chinese issue of such maps ought therefore, in the interests of good relations, to be discontinued. But it was not, of course, the maps that mattered. It was the Chinese refusal either to disavow them or, if these unacceptable claims were serious, to explain why they had not admitted as much from the beginning.

The maps were not to be disavowed, or withdrawn, or corrected. Nor were they to be confirmed at this point as representing official territorial claims, though Chou En-lai now moved nearer to that position. What he had once shrugged aside as the uncorrected pretensions of a previous Chinese régime emerged (23 January 1959) as the possible basis of a Chinese demand for 'surveys and consultations'. It could no longer be denied that the maps had a function in Chinese political strategy. As a counter to Nehru's proposition that there was 'no major boundary dispute between China and India' their function was to open and keep open a dispute throughout the entire length of the frontier.

On areas of local disagreement, such as Barahoti, these early exchanges between the two Prime Ministers presented an appearance of accord on methods of peaceful settlement. Even here, however, it could be seen that by 'preserving the *status quo*' pending negotiations the Chinese meant the retention of control where they had advanced, while the Indians meant vacation by both sides or return to the *status quo ante*. On the major and general issue the entire Chinese approach was towards an indefinite enlargement of the area of dispute and an indefinite postponement of a settlement.

Of the discernible motives for this policy, one was in a sense juridical. This was the Chinese desire to secure their very questionable rights in Tibet by something more than the Trade and Intercourse Agreement with India. A frontier-question could, or even should, have been discussed in those negotiations if one existed, and Nehru had enquired in his first letter why the Chinese had not wished to raise the matter. It was, replied Chou En-lai, 'because conditions were not yet ripe for its settlement and the Chinese side, on its part, had had no time to study the question'. It had now 'proceeded to take certain steps in making preparations'. These, it is clear, would entail in the first place the invalidation of all previous treaties or understandings in which Tibet had exercised a negotiating capacity of its own. In theory, of course, the Chinese People's Government might then agree to a frontier-alignment substantially the same as the existing one, much as the Indian Government had been able to retain some of its predecessors' privileges in Tibet by differently-worded conventions with her new Chinese rulers. But it is unlikely that the Trade and Intercourse talks would have got very far if Peking had introduced a prior condition which questioned the historical legality of India's northern frontiers. Sooner or later this policy of repudiation would further have involved Sikkim and Bhutan, and the clearly affirmed Indian relations with those Himalayan States. For this the time must indeed have seemed unripe in 1954. It was not ripe yet, but the 'preparations' hinted at by Chou En-lai may well have included the intensive efforts of Chinese Communist propaganda and subversion carried into those Tibetan outposts in the intervening years.

It was the design of cutting away the past treaty-position of Tibet, as much as of India, that brought to the startled notice of Nehru, in Chou's letter of 23 January 1959, the Chinese Communist contention that 'historically no treaty or agreement on the Sino-Indian boundary has ever been concluded between the Chinese central Government and the Indian Government'. This, though wholly negative, was virtually the first sign from Mao's Peking of any interest in the pre-Communist history of the subject. In reply Nehru gave notice of an Indian reliance on documentary evidence by drawing attention to particular treaties. And on the Simla Conventions of 1914 he recorded the important point that the Chinese Government's repudiation of its plenipotentiary's agreement to the McMahon Line had been wholly in respect of the China-Tibet boundary and never in respect of the northern boundary of India and Burma. When his letter was answered after the lapse of several eventful months the point was not directly met. But Chou En-lai had already, on 23 January, widened the breach in the McMahon Line which he had made (from the Chinese viewpoint) two years earlier by bringing the subject within the scope of discussion. The McMahon Line was now ('as you are aware') a product 'of the British policy of aggression against the Tibet Region of China' and was not to be considered legal. And Chou's personal assurances on the subject had become: 'The Chinese Government on the one hand finds it necessary to take a more or less realistic attitude towards the McMahon Line and, on the other hand, cannot but act with prudence and needs time to deal with the matter.' How was this prudence to be exercised during an indefinite postponement of the recognition previously offered? Presumably, in a Chinese assessment of the 'friendly attitude' of the Indian Government which had been attached as a condition. And the most immediate test of Indian behaviour was developing in the growing threat of disaster and exposure for the Chinese Communists in Tibet. In Peking it must have been painfully obvious that India was well placed to take advantage of the coming storm. Intervention across the frontier, direct or indirect, would have been expected of an Imperialist Power and in similar circumstances would have been recommended in Maoist strategy to a Communist Power. Even on the most sanguine estimate of Indian non-alignment there would have been a risk to be covered, and the Chinese Communists were no more given than their predecessors to exaggerating the political virtues of their neighbours. The frontier-policy developed towards India at this time seemed calculated to exert the maximum of pressure with the minimum of commitment.

A third use for an open frontier-problem can be surmized from the first tentative reference, in Chou En-lai's letter of 23 January, to the special importance attached by the Chinese to their territorial requirements in the western sector, i.e. to the as yet undefined claim covering their military road. In itself this was far too oblique to be taken as the opening bid for an exchange of territories. It is doubtful, indeed, whether at this stage the Chinese had decided how much of Ladakh would meet their eventual needs. Here, as elsewhere, a settled frontier was envisaged as a distant, not an urgent prospect. But it is from this point that the practice of associating the situation in Ladakh with their hardening claims south of the Mc-Mahon Line became more and more evident in Chinese frontier-arguments, with a consequent resistance to any Indian effort to treat either question separately. That India would ever have allowed its title to the North-East Frontier Agency to be converted into a Chinese concession is almost impossible to believe. But this does not mean that the principle of territorial exchanges was ruled out; and before the question had been driven beyond the hope of public acquiescence, a number of possibilities appear to have been considered in Delhi. The most reasonable was a suggestion of relinquishing Indian claims to the Aksai Chin in return for an Indian acquisition of the Chumbi Valley, which interposes Tibetan territory between Sikkim and Bhutan in a highly inconvenient manner and is in physical terms an invasion of the general watershed line. This project did not reach the point of negotiation. And in the absence of at least a broad Chinese acceptance of an existing frontier, it might have been expected to come up against the argument used by Chou En-lai in the Burmese question—that 'one part of China cannot be exchanged for another'.

VI

EFFECTS OF THE TIBET
CRISIS: 1959–60

THE POLITICAL CLIMATE

In March 1959 the inhabitants of Lhasa, suspecting a Chinese intention to place the person of the Dalai Lama under military control, joined cause with the spreading national revolt led by Kham tribesmen. An inevitable consequence of the explosion was increased tension along the southern frontier of Tibet, with the probability of further incidents. At the same time events tended to support the Indian view that any Sino-Indian frontier-problem was a problem of such incidents and intrusions alone, and not of a doubtful or unestablished boundary. The Dalai Lama, escaping with his closest advisers, sought refuge in India as his predecessors had done in times of crisis. He knew the point of his crossing of the McMahon Line, a little east of Bhutan at Chhuthangmo, and he was there received by an Indian official. Many thousands of Tibetan refugees finding their way through wild country into India, Bhutan, Sikkim and Nepal, knew when they had reached safety. During three months in which India was fiercely charged by Chinese propaganda with interference in Tibet there was no reported frontier-disturbance. Several factors might account for this, but it suggested at least a rough and common knowledge of where the frontier lay.

The official exchanges that did take place between Peking and Delhi in the period immediately following the revolt were in other, and political, fields. India and the world at large were left in no doubt of the nature of China's political grievances against her neighbour in relation to Tibetan developments. But the full force of this attack was confined, with evident deliberation, to the Chinese propaganda-machine. Even the Indian Government's compliance with the Dalai Lama's request for political asylum, which was to become a major cause of Chinese complaint, received no official acknowledgment or comment when communicated to the Chinese Ambassador on 3 April. Chou En-lai himself kept out of the picture. Nehru's last letter to him on the frontier-issue (22 March) remained unanswered for several months, and his own public references to India in reporting on Tibetan affairs were comparatively restrained. Meanwhile the Chinese press and radio offensive culminated on 6 May in a key *People's Daily* article criticizing the Indian Prime Minister from an ideological standpoint. The article was headed 'The Revolution in Tibet and Nehru's Philosophy'. The campaign was then, for the time being, switched off. But the continuity of the Chinese Communist approach was to be strikingly demonstrated two and a half years later, when the Chinese accompanied their military invasion of India with the publication of what the *People's Daily* called the second instalment of the same article.

This 1959 campaign had evidently a twofold function, apart from any genuine element it may have embodied of belief in Indian responsibility for the Chinese setback in Tibet. The damage to both Chinese and Communist prestige had been very serious. To the emergent Asian nations it had been revealed that eight years of Chinese effort had failed to commend Communist ideas or processes to a people supposed to have been groaning under feudalism. At the same time the form and strength of the Tibetan protest had a nationalist aspect that morally demolished China's claims to sovereignty. The reaction in countries of Buddhist sympathies was a special problem, but respect for religious freedom in general caused an even wider revulsion, especially as the Chinese counter-measures became known or rumoured. And in the re-latively closed world of the Communist bloc, where such ideas were not expressed, Peking nevertheless became aware that it was criticized for blundering and failure. For all of this only one excuse was possible: powerful, external, imperialist instigation. The first Chinese allegations of direct intervention by the U.S.A. and the Chiang Kai-shek régime carried little conviction in proportion to the scale of the affair. Only an India conceived as subservient to imperialism and hostile to China could fill the necessary rôle.

THE POLITICAL CHALLENGE

The second function of Chinese propaganda at this time was that of notifying the Indian Government of the basis on which serious Chinese hostility could, if necessary, be established. 'Interference in China's domestic affairs' was broadened, on this showing, into a matter of political attitudes, ideological viewpoints, and expressions of public or private opinion. In particular India was warned against using the valuable hostage which she might seem to have acquired in the Dalai Lama. None of this, at the present stage, was given the form of strictly attributable Chinese policy. Frontier-questions and territorial demands were not mentioned, and the Prime Ministers' correspondence remained unresumed. The definitive trial of India's political colour took the form of what India later called a 'state-ment', and China an 'appeal', which the Chinese Am-bassador in Delhi lodged with the Indian Foreign Secretary on 16 May 1959.

The first half-dozen paragraphs of this document con-veyed in strong terms a series of Chinese complaints. The charges of Indian interference in Tibet, already publicized by Chinese organs and rejected by the Indian Prime Minister in Parliament, were now repeated at an official level. It was shown that the Chinese Government took exception, not only to the granting of political asylum to the Dalai Lama and to Nehru's meeting with him ('giving a welcome to a Chinese rebel'), but also to 'slanders' uttered in Indian parliamentary debate and in the Indian press. An incidental case of disfigurement of a portrait of Mao Tse-tung occurring in a Bombay demonstration was resurrected as a serious insult on which the Indian Govern-ment had failed to give a satisfactory reply. 'Words and deeds' had become 'intolerable', and were not to be excused 'by recourse to any pretext, whether "freedom of speech" or any other "freedoms".'

The final paragraph appealed for an Indian understand-ing of the conditions for future good relations between the two countries. What was required was India's recognition of a Chinese 'policy of struggle' concentrated upon 'the vicious and aggressive U.S. imperialism'. The rebellion in Tibet would be dealt with without endangering India—'you can wait and see'. The state policy of China was that 'we cannot have two centres of attention, nor can we take friend for foe'. If non-aligned India would similarly recognize that 'you cannot have two fronts . . . here lies the meeting-point of our two sides'.

On 23 May the Indian Government returned a firm

reply to this document, asserting the freedom of expression in India, the sovereignty of the Indian Parliament, the rights of the Indian people (as of the Chinese) to a Government of their choice, and the refusal of that Government to 'discard or vary any of their own policies under any pressure from outside'.

There had been no mention of the frontier in this exchange, but it had established the political context in which any dispute would be conducted. India had failed, under direct challenge, to pass the test of 'friendly relations' to which the previous show of Chinese acommodation had been attached. The 'appropriate time' had thus arrived, not for a frontier-settlement but for the official declaration of a dispute.

PEKING WIDENS THE DISPUTE

This came in a continuation by Chou En-lai of the correspondence resting with Nehru's letter of 22 March. But it did not come immediately. The summer months were punctuated by Indian representations in regard to the harassment of Indian nationals in Tibet, restrictions on India's official agencies there, and interference with Bhutanese rights of communication across the Chumbi Valley. It seems reasonable to assume that the Chinese Prime Minister was awaiting any occasion of frontier-protest that might occur with the return of the freer patrolling-season in the Himalayas. But other preoccupations doubtless played their part. Unrest in Sinkiang, catching fire from the Tibetan rising, had become serious at a time when the new Chinese communications were constantly threatened, if not actually cut, by rebel forces. Soviet diplomacy was making headway in southern Asia in unpublicized rivalry with the Chinese. Peking looked askance at Soviet moves towards a measure of détente with the U.S.A., while Moscow offered less than full support for China's activation of ideological conflict across her border in Laos.

At the end of July an Indian patrol was captured by Chinese in the Pangong Lake area in the southern part of the Ladakh-Tibet frontier. Other incidents had been reported from the east, and it was in the McMahon Line section of the frontier that the first use of fire-arms occurred on 25 August. Disputes as to the situation of the Indian post at Longju, south of Migyitun, notwithstanding, it was a Chinese force which attacked it, causing the Indian picket to withdraw after one man had been killed and another wounded.

This action, at all events, was sufficiently definite to be interpreted by the Soviet Government (as was revealed much later) as a deliberate Chinese provocation aimed at increasing international tension to the detriment of the Krushchev-Eisenhower talks at Camp David. A *Tass* statement regretting Sino-Indian frontier-tension accordingly followed on 9 September. The neutral tone of the comment from China's Communist ally caused serious offence in Peking, and it had been in the course of Chinese efforts to have it modified or suppressed that the Soviet Chargé d'Affaires had been shown a copy of Chou En-lai's long-delayed letter to Nehru, drafted but not yet transmitted. The attempt failing, the letter went on its way, with the date 8 September. And it was this letter which at last began to offer statements 'to prove that the Sino-Indian boundary has never been formally delimited'.

The basic Chinese hypothesis was ideological. China and India, as 'countries which were long subjected to imperialist aggression', ought 'naturally to hold an identical view' of the historical background to the question. It ought to be agreed, that is to say, that in the past, 'using India as its base, Britain conducted extensive territorial expansion into China's Tibet region, and even the Sinkiang region'. For India to have accepted this reading of history would indeed have left it to the Chinese to decide what fruits of imperialist aggression they required her to disgorge. Taken in conjunction with the Chinese demand that the entire 2,000-mile frontier be renegotiated, it would leave India entirely dependent, in any such negotiation, on the Chinese proposal to adopt a 'more or less realistic attitude' and to take into account 'the friendly relations between China and India'. And there was a warning of the likely operation of Chinese 'realism' in Chou En-lai's remark that border-incidents up to this point in which India had been prepared to recognize two areas as disputed—had been 'caused wholly by the trespassing of Indian troops'. At the same time frontier-questions were given a significantly political context by the complaint that since the rebellion in Tibet 'many political figures and propaganda organs in India have seized the occasion to make a great deal of anti-Chinese utterances'.

The subject of the McMahon Line was handled by Chou En-lai in two distinct ways. On the one hand a Chinese claim to the whole area south of the Line down to the edge of the Brahmaputra Valley was now expressed unequivocally, and with an ironical echo of Nehru's refusal to consider the surrender of large parts of India. Wrote Chou:

This piece of territory corresponds in size to the Chekiang Province of China and is as big as 90,000 square kilometres. Mr Prime Minister, how could China agree to accept under coercion such an illegal line which would have it relinquish its rights and disgrace itself by selling out its territory—and such a large piece of territory at that?

On the other hand the McMahon Line boundary was used as a reference in charging that Indian patrol-forces, at Longju and elsewhere, had 'overstepped' it. The Longju incident was not interpreted as the appearance of Indian personnel a hundred or so miles within Chinese territory. It was 'the first instance of armed clash *along the Sino-Indian border*'. The possibility of treating the eastern sector of the Sino-Indian boundary as a matter of small adjustments in the McMahon Line seemed thus to be retained. But the pressure of Chinese territorial ambitions was simultaneously built up in a way which no Indian Government responsible to an elected legislature could have failed to resist.

It was at this point that the Indian Government, rather belatedly as it might seem, had met that responsibility by laying before Parliament, on 7 September, the first of what was to become a long series of White Papers periodically setting out notes, memoranda and letters exchanged between Peking and Delhi. The previous restriction of publicity had been adopted in the interests of preventing tension and facilitating diplomacy. But the Tibetan developments in general, and the border-clash at Longju in particular, had produced a state of public awareness in India which could no longer be ignored. The new policy reduced the Indian Government's scope for manœuvre in the dispute, while the Chinese Government continued to operate in conditions of rigid Communist control of information and public expression. But it also made possible in India the unity of democratic support essential for meeting the growing crisis. With the facts made public even the Communist Party of India found itself reluctantly, and with much inner dispute, drawn into the path which was to lead to an official condemnation of the Chinese Communist Government.

In the result the next frontier-clash, the serious incident near the Kongka Pass in Ladakh towards the end of October, became public knowledge in India more quickly than the Chinese seem to have expected. At all events the ten members of a party of Indian frontier-police, captured after an engagement in which nine others had been killed, were held under severe conditions and exploited for a Chinese propaganda-operation. This otherwise pointless tactic (since the survivors were finally restored to Indian custody) can plausibly be linked with the energetic efforts which Peking was then making to explain confidentially to Moscow that the trouble on the frontier had been provoked by 'Indian reactionaries'. In this they were unsuccessful, and when Khrushchev mentioned the Sino-Indian dispute in the Supreme Soviet on 31 October he offered no support to the Chinese viewpoint, merely hoping that frontier-incidents would not be repeated and that any questions in dispute would be solved 'by friendly negotiations to the mutual satisfaction of both sides'. In India official and public reactions to the Kongka Pass affair were naturally strong, especially when the full particulars became available to Parliament on 15 December.

PROPOSALS AND COUNTER-PROPOSALS

Two years and nine months were to pass (October 1959 to July 1962) before the next exchange of shots, again in Ladakh. But the position in the latter months of 1959 is of great importance to the elucidation of a Chinese frontier-policy which was to culminate in invasion, withdrawal and stalemate. On 26 September, before the

Kongka Pass clash (forty to fifty miles inside a well-established point on the Ladakh boundary), Nehru had replied to Chou En-lai at length and in detail, with further particulars of the Indian frontier-justification supplied in an annexure. On 4 November, after the clash, a note from the Indian Ministry of External Affairs to the Chinese Ambassador pointed out, among other things, that the Indian Prime Minister's letter remained unanswered except by aggression. On 7 November the Chinese Prime Minister acknowledged it briefly, and offered in terms of urgency a proposal for effectively maintaining 'the *status quo* of the border', and for tranquillizing it as a preliminary to 'a friendly settlement'.

This proposal of 7 November, of which more was to be heard, was for a twenty-kilometre (twelve-mile) withdrawal of the 'armed forces' of both sides, in the eastern sector from the McMahon Line and in the western sector from 'the line up to which each side exercises actual control'.

The prompt Indian reply, in Nehru's letter of 16 November, was in the form of a counter-proposal which distinguished between the eastern and western sectors in regard both to the character of the disagreement and to the actual situation. The Indian Prime Minister also stated categorically that until quite recently India's armed forces had not been committed to the protection of the northern frontier. 'Our border check-posts were manned by civil constabulary, equipped with light arms.' Only after 'the recent unfortunate incidents' had responsibility been transferred to the military authorities.

On the McMahon Line section of the frontier the conditions were held by Nehru to be such that all risk of border-clashes could be eliminated if each Government instructed its outposts not to send out patrols. Longju, however, presented a special case. The Indian conviction that the post was south of the boundary was opposed by the Chinese. But wherever the place was it had been the Chinese armed forces which attacked it, and no interim arrangement which left them in possession was acceptable to India. The Indian request for a Chinese evacuation of the post was therefore repeated, the undertaking being added that in that case 'we on our part will not reoccupy it'. Eventually, and quietly, the Chinese fell in with this suggestion.

In the western sector the Chinese proposal of a twenty-kilometre withdrawal from 'the line of actual control' established by Chinese advances would of course have left the Chinese well within the Indian frontiers as India understood them. The actual extent of Chinese claims in the area was still not known in India with any precision; but the immediate question was the interim avoidance of clashes, and it was essential (wrote Nehru) that 'we do not get involved in interminable discussions on the *status quo* at this stage'. He therefore proposed that in this sector the Chinese should withdraw to the east of the Ladakh frontier as officially claimed and indicated by India, while the Indians withdrew to the west of the frontier shown in China's 1956 map, representing the latest Chinese claim of which the Indian Government had knowledge. Thus a temporary no-man's-land would be created in an area of dispute which, being 'almost entirely uninhabited', did not necessitate the presence of administrative personnel.

For the accepted purpose of tranquillization the pro-posal had clearly much to commend it. But it took no account of the Aksai Chin road and the value that the Chinese might set upon it. It therefore drew Chou En-lai to come forward, on 17 December, with an account of the undisturbed construction of the road as 'eloquent proof that the area has indeed always been under Chinese jurisdiction'. He also continued to insist on equating the issues of the eastern and western sectors in any approach to negotiations and in any temporary measures to reduce tension.

It was of no less significance that Chou En-lai, from 7 November, was pressing hard for a meeting with Nehru. He continued to do so, without modifying a basic Chinese approach which he knew to be unacceptable, and without responding to the Indian view that the manifest disagreement on the facts of the case must be tackled before any frontier-discussions could be usefully undertaken. An accord of some kind was evidently an objective of the Chinese Communists at this time, and some part of the extreme position they had adopted was intended for use as threat or inducement to achieve that objective. The accord was to be sought in private discussion between the two Prime Ministers as a matter of urgency—at a week's notice, Chou suggested on 17 December. Peking was the first preference for a meeting-place, Rangoon the second. The factual examination which interested India was if possible to be sidestepped. What Chou En-lai wanted was to establish 'agreement of principles as guidance to concrete discussion'. Since Nehru perceived no basis of discussion in the position to which the Chinese Government was ostensibly determined to adhere, he was plainly less eager than Chou En-lai for a personal confrontation. Consequently the meeting did not take place until the following April (1960), and then in Delhi. In the meantime China's frontier-relations with certain other countries had thrown further light on the nature of her policies.

VII

FRONTIER FENCE-MENDING:
1959-61

THE SETTLEMENT WITH BURMA

THE security of her southern frontiers would appear at this time as the most logical Chinese requirement. Whether such security was achievable, in Chinese Communist eyes, by the establishment of settled boundaries, and if so on what terms, are separate questions. Up to the end of the critical year of 1959, no new boundary-negotiation had anywhere been concluded by the Chinese People's Government, which in 1949 had declared a general intention of re-examining past treaties and in 1955, at Bandung, a particular readiness to stabilize its frontiers. The only neighbour with whom discussions had proceeded was Burma, and at Burma's request.

In June 1959, with the long argument still undetermined, the new Burmese Prime Minister, General Ne Win, had sent to Peking a set of proposals representing the agreed position of the Burmese parties. The Chinese reply avoided taking the matter further. Ne Win stiffened his position as a 'non-partisan Prime Minister', and described his own approach as a compromise embodying the maximum offer that Burma could make. While Chou En-lai was endeavouring to lure Nehru to Peking without abating Chinese demands, Ne Win had offered to visit Peking without abating his own. The suggestion was accepted on 2 December. Ne Win arrived with a delegation on 23 January 1960. An agreement was signed

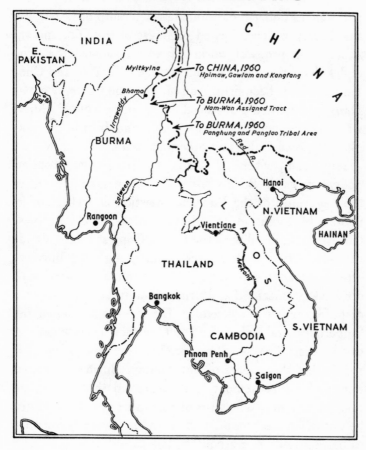

To CHINA, 1960
Hpimaw, Gawlam and Kangfang

To BURMA, 1960
Nam-Wan Assigned Tract

To BURMA, 1960
Panghung and Panglao Tribal Area

7. South-East Asia

on 28 January. 'In five days,' writes Miss Woodman, 'General Ne Win had secured for his country the frontier which had been claimed all along, with differences only of square miles in the Hpimaw area and in that of Panghung-Panglao which were left for a joint committee to settle on the spot.'*

The agreement had still to be debated in the Burmese

* Dorothy Woodman: *The Making of Burma* (op. cit.).

127

parliament, under the resumed premiership of U Nu. But the Treaty which followed on 1 October 1960, and the survey and protocol work thereafter, showed the principles that had been resolved between Ne Win and Chou En-lai to have been firm. And of them the Peking *People's Daily* had pointedly observed (1 February 1960): 'Surely what has happened between China and Burma can take place between China and other countries.'

Any comparison of Chinese Communist frontier-policies towards Burma and India must take account of the beginning of the Burmese question as well as of its manner of resolution. It had been opened by the Burmese Government, faced with the fact of Chinese forces astride the boundary. To that extent, and though the Burmese often negotiated stubbornly, the case remained at China's disposal. It meant that Burma initially acknowledged a dispute, implicitly conceding that the boundaries of the 'imperialist era' (which had not, in fact, everywhere received their final seal) required to be renegotiated. It meant that the leaders of independent Burma petitioned Peking for a settlement, and journeyed thither to state their case. The vassal-status of a Chinese neighbour might be outmoded and repudiated, without ceasing altogether to be politically operative.

On the other hand India, so far from asking the Chinese Communist Government for a settlement, had been satisfied with the validity of her frontier and had said so. The development of a *Panch Shila* relationship with China, while it was expected by India to facilitate the peaceful settlement of local boundary-differences if they should arise, presumed a joint acceptance of the frontier in its general alignment and its legal basis. The Chinese tactics were therefore concentrated, and in a manner which the Indians

found lacking in candour, upon the objective of man-
œuvring the Indian Government into recognizing that the
frontier was in dispute and into asking for a settlement to
be negotiated. But even with Chinese forces inside the
borders as India understood them, and the Chinese Government taking a stand on this '*status quo*', the Indian
Government was not to be trapped into relinquishing its
inherited authority on the ideological grounds adopted
and pressed by Communist China. An equal alertness had
been shown in the rejection of every Chinese move to
question or modify India's non-aligned position and the
independent control of her policies. As early as 1950 a
Chinese suggestion that the Indian Government had been
'affected by foreign influences hostile to China in Tibet'
had been sharply rejected. In May 1959 the Chinese
invitation for an alignment of Indian political attitudes
with those of China had been still more clearly and firmly
turned down. Yet the Chou-Nehru correspondence
showed the Chinese Prime Minister, subtle by comparison
with the crude efforts of his Ambassador, injecting similar
assumptions into the issues of the Sino-Indian boundaries.
It might be concluded that some, at all events, of the
principles which Chou urgently wished to consolidate in
private talks with Nehru 'as guidance to concrete discussions' were of this nature. When this again produced
nothing but an Indian insistence on first establishing the
facts of the frontier by investigation, other methods of
reducing India's stature in a political confrontation with
Communist China were tried. The most extreme of these
was the massive Chinese invasion, followed by almost
contemptuous withdrawal, in the last months of 1962.

China's Indian problem was inevitably not only different from, but very much larger than, her problem with

Burma. India was a major Asian power, a potential rival both nationally and ideologically, and a State to which even the hazy traditions of vassalage could not be attached. For neighbours of roughly the Burmese size and situation Chinese Communist diplomacy evolved a special instrument of relationship in the Treaty of Friendship and Mutual Non-Aggression. This was the price exacted from Ne Win for a Chinese endorsement of the frontiers 'left over from history', and duly paid by Nu with the loudly acclaimed ceremonies of signature at the next anniversary of the Peking régime. Though fairly innocuous in most of its wording, its effect was to restrict the scope of an independent Burmese policy, domestic and foreign, and to open channels of Chinese penetration and influence.

'BUFFER-ZONES' IN CHINESE POLICY

In this aspect the final and sudden conclusion of the question which Burma had raised some ten years earlier contained a certain logic, one conception of national security being traded for another. The Burmese saw security in a settled and guaranteed frontier, the Chinese in a relationship which accepted their own influence in a neighbour country and excluded that of others. The old word 'vassal' and the new word 'satellite' were not to be mentioned. The term 'buffer-state', when picked up by Peking from some Indian newspaper-comment on the Tibetan question, had been violently denounced as a device of imperialism. But at the same time China was expressing an increasing interest in establishing around her frontiers areas which would serve her, in all but name, as 'buffer-zones'.

Mao Tse-tung had himself talked much of 'intermediate zones' in his early lucubrations on the struggle between capitalist and communist systems, and his notions were to be revived as polemical texts in 1963. In 1958 a suggestion had been made by Nehru for an international area in Asia from which atomic weapons would be excluded. This received some Chinese support, and considerably more from 1959 onwards after the un-revealed Soviet refusal to provide the Chinese with a sample nuclear bomb and technical particulars. The con-cept of nuclear-free zones received varying and oppor-tunistic Chinese support. But the earlier, and more particular, publicity for 'zones of peace' had been used in extenuation of Communist China's desired relationship with her neighbours. In 1954, for instance, reporting on his first tour of Asian capitals, Chou En-lai had declared China's concern to 'establish an area of collective peace in Indo-China and its surrounding countries', and to extend it further in Asia if favourable conditions appeared. By July 1955, after Bandung, he found this aim to be 'realistic and attainable'.

In the definition of these border-zones it was stipu-lated that the countries included in them should maintain 'neutrality' and reject any participation in military blocs or coalitions (Communist China's military alliance with the USSR notwithstanding). In notes exchanged with the Indian Government on the frontier-question China's need to create 'the most peaceful, secure and friendly border zones' was said to be fundamental. With Burma a buffer-zone was achieved in the Treaty of Friendship and Mutual Non-Aggression. With Nepal the achievement was less. But the attempt was notable.

NEGOTIATING WITH NEPAL

In one respect Nepal was very much more open than India to Chinese frontier-pressure. An agreement 'to maintain the friendly relations between the Chinese People's Republic and the Kingdom of Nepal, and on trade and intercourse between the Tibet region of China and Nepal' had been signed in Katmandu on 20 September 1956, two-and-a-half years after the Sino-Indian trade-agreement on Tibet. It settled similar matters, substituting reciprocal trade-agencies for Nepal's former special privileges in Tibet. But in abrogating all former treaties, including those between Tibet and Nepal, it removed the 1856 authority for Nepal's northern frontier without specifically providing a new one. The previous delimitation, though it lacked definition in the almost unapproachable alignment of the central Himalayas, had been undisputed for a century, except in three small areas.

On the other hand, Nepal was not a country to be treated with disrespect, as the Chinese had historic reasons to appreciate. To its former assets of difficult terrain and military prowess it had now added an internationally recognized independence enabling its Prime Minister Koirala to declare, when events in Tibet brought Chinese armies to the frontier, that Nepal would resist any Chinese invasion (4 October 1959). Next month he added in an interview: 'If we are invaded we have our army ... 20,000 men, poorly armed perhaps, but suitable for our terrain – to stem the first attack until the United Nations can act.'

No question of the frontier had then been openly raised, either by Nepal or by China. Koirala admitted in the Nepalese Parliament at this time that certain old differences existed, but declared that there was no new dispute and played down the strongly current reports of local Chinese incursions. Diplomatic relations with the Chinese People's Government had been established only in 1955, but there was no Chinese Embassy in Katmandu.

Peking's Ambassador to India held the concurrent post, and the Nepalese Ambassador to China was also resident in Delhi. To supplement this unsatisfactory channel of influence, there were promises, largely unfulfilled, of Chinese aid, and an active China-Nepal Friendship Association. For a few months in 1957 the premiership had been held by an allegedly pro-Communist leader, Dr K. I. Singh, who had been in exile in China and had obliquely revealed that he had been offered, and had rejected, military support to 'liberate' Nepal. But Nepal's parliamentary Government was still, at the turn of 1959–1960, controlled by a Congress Party friendly to India. India had her Treaty of Friendship, a military mission and civilian advisers in Nepal, considerable aid undertakings and the only road-connection. There was, further, the Indian declaration of a fundamental interest in the defence of Nepal's northern frontier.

There was thus much which offended the Chinese view of appropriate relations with border-States, and which a Chinese Treaty of Friendship and Mutual Non-Aggression with Nepal might help to remove. But the element of an Indian 'presence' in Nepal (traditionally suspicious of both neighbouring powers) was itself a point of weakness on which the Chinese Communist diplomacy could play. For this the first need was to reduce or obscure the more obvious menace of Chinese forces operating close to Nepal's northern frontier. The Nepalese Government's policy of denying all reports of actual Chinese intrusions offered an opening; and on 11 March 1960, Prime Minister Koirala was welcomed with much publicity on 'a friendly visit' to the Chinese People's Republic. The purpose was not defined, and Koirala repeated to a Peking mass-rally the warning that territorial aggression by 'any power-mad nation, however big and powerful' would 'lead to a complete disturbance of global peace'. This, also, was the occasion on which Nepalese students in Peking brought to his notice the Liu Pei-hua *Brief History*, with its apparently vast irredentist claims to a Chinese Empire in which Nepal figured as a minute component. The Koirala-Chou communiqué of 21 March, however, indicated discussion and agreement on an important range of topics.

The Chinese Government had proposed the conclusion of a Treaty of Peace and Friendship between the two countries, and the Chinese Prime Minister was to visit Nepal to discuss and to sign it. The 1956 agreement had been taken further by a mutual undertaking for embassies to be established in Peking and Katmandu. And an agreement of principles in 'the question of the boundary between the two countries' had been separately signed.

The basis for delineating the frontier would be 'the traditional customary line'. Apart from discrepancies in certain sections, the understanding of this line by both Governments was stated to be broadly similar, and demarcation on the ground would be carried out after a joint committee had reached decisions by means of surveys and on-the-spot investigations in controversial areas. In such areas, if 'the state of actual jurisdiction' was not in dispute, the adjustment of map-differences would take account of natural features, including 'watersheds, valleys, passes, etc.' Where actual jurisdiction was in dispute, joint teams would ascertain the facts of the situation. The boundary would then be determined by adjustments 'in accordance with the principles of equality, mutual benefit, friendship and mutual accommodation'.

In addition to the small but long-standing differences to which Koirala had previously referred, he found in

Peking what he described as a new claim by the Chinese Communists (though there had in fact been evidence of it in Chinese publications in 1958). This was for the inclusion of Mount Everest within Chinese territory. Koirala had summarily rejected it, he said on returning to Katmandu, and so there had been no discussion. But the point continued to rankle. A proposal attributed to Mao Tse-tung that Everest should be renamed 'Nepal-China Friendship Peak' was followed by a Peking claim that Chinese climbers had scaled the mountain (without the customary permission from Nepal) and placed on the summit a bust of Mao wrapped in a Chinese flag. Even after the signing of the Sino-Nepalese Boundary Treaty (5 October 1961) the question remained in doubt.

By the Koirala-Chou agreements of 21 March 1960, Nepal was also to receive from China over the next three years a new 'free grant of economic aid without any conditions or privileges attached'—but providing for the admission of Chinese technicians to Nepal, which the earlier aid agreement of 1956 had expressly precluded. What the Chinese had not got was the inclusion of a 'Mutual Non-Aggression' undertaking which would have restricted Nepalese foreign policy, effectively excluded Indian military assistance, and nullified India's unilateral guarantee of Nepal's northern frontier.

As with Burma, the Chinese were now moving quickly. A month after his Peking talks with Koirala, Chou En-lai suffered a set-back in Delhi, where the confrontation at last achieved with Nehru produced, not an Indian submission to his 'points of principle' but a reluctant Chinese acquiescence in a joint factual investigation of the frontier-question. But from Delhi Chou flew to Katmandu to finalize the Treaty of Peace and Friendship with Nepal

THE FRONTIERS OF CHINA

(26–9 April 1960). Vice-Premier Chen Yi, who accompanied him, celebrated the signature of the Treaty with an expression of particular thanks to Nepal for 'not bullying China'. It was clear that friendly boundary-agreements with Burma and Nepal (achieved by the Chinese Government's acceptance of principles which it rejected in the case of India) were to be used for the isolation of the Indian Government as an intransigent renegade from 'the Bandung spirit'. And at the end of June, while the Indian investigation-team was engaged with the Chinese in the first difficult session in Peking, one of the most striking demonstrations of partiality in Chinese tactics was provided in a serious frontier-incident with Nepal. Near Mustang an unarmed Nepalese observation-party, investigating the presence of a large Chinese military force on the Nepal side of what was supposed to be a demilitarized boundary, was captured and its leader killed. When Katmandu protested, the Chinese Government made unprecedented efforts to restore good relations, expressing deep regrets, attributing the affair to the 'carelessness of certain low-ranking Chinese personnel', paying immediately a sizeable sum in compensation and offering undertakings for the future.

A few months later the situation in Nepal was transformed by the coup of 15 December 1960, in which King Mahendra assumed direct rule of his country, overthrowing the Koirala Government. This appeared as a serious blow to Indian influence, and Indian concern for the undemocratic nature of the action was answered by a sustained anti-Indian campaign in the Nepalese press. It was to be several years before the breach could be restored, and the advantage to the Chinese appeared to be immediate. The swift endorsement of the King's coup by the small

Nepalese Communist Party suggested that Communist China would have little, if any, compunction in dealing with a royal dictatorship in place of a social-democratic régime. This proved to be the case. The exploitation of Nepalese suspicions of India took an increasing place in Chinese propaganda, and Nepalese traders and nationals in Tibet, who had hitherto been oppressed equally with Indian nationals by the Chinese authorities, began to receive more favoured treatment. In the boundary-discussions, however, there were signs of some slowing-up on the part of China. For King Mahendra, whatever the present state of his relations with India, had hedged the approach to China by strengthening his country's links with Britain, the United States and Soviet Russia. He had also pronounced firmly on Nepal's territorial integrity (including possession of Mount Everest).

The King's visit to Peking to sign the Boundary Treaty with the Chinese Head of State, Liu Shao-chi, took place in October 1961, a year after the Sino-Burmese Boundary Treaty and a few days before U Nu himself returned to Peking to sign boundary-protocols for Burma. Both events were highly publicized by the Chinese, whose official speeches attributed frontier-problems between China and her neighbours to the machinations of aggressive imperialism, so that their solution in particular cases could suggest anti-imperialist solidarity. King Mahendra, however, in a public appearance pointedly ignored the assertion by Peng Chen (Mayor of Peking and member of the Chinese Politburo) that their two countries were united by 'a common will' against 'imperialist aggression'. He revealed instead that Liu Shao Chi had been brought in their talks to admit that 'like all big Powers, China might have the tendency to ignore' the rights of smaller nations. Liu had assured him, said the King, that his Government would 'take meticulous care to avoid the repetition of such blunders'.

As an additional insurance, Nepal had kept clear of a 'Mutual Non-Aggression' pact with China, retaining a freedom to repair her relations with India which was eventually used. This was important in the field of communications, since the economic talks during the King's visit had included an agreement for the completion of a strategic road-link between Lhasa and Katmandu by the summer of 1966. The framework of this and other agreements on Chinese material and technical aid to be supplied to Nepal continued to be of a markedly less restrictive character than that which Peking had succeeded in imposing on Burma.

AFGHANISTAN AND PAKISTAN

Two other independent States, adjacent to China's frontier-zone in a small but important, and long-disputed, sector, were Afghanistan and Pakistan. During Peking's fence-mending operations of 1960–1, Afghanistan was linked with China in a Treaty of Friendship and Mutual Non-Aggression without any raising of the frontier-question; while Pakistan, which had notified its willingness to settle the question of its 'undemarcated' boundary with China, continued to be very guardedly treated.

Afghanistan had recognized the Chinese People's Republic in 1949, and Ambassadors were exchanged early in 1955. Two years later, in a first visit to Kabul, Chou En-lai mentioned that there was a common border (in fact created by the Anglo-Russian-Afghan Pamir settlement which the Chinese had frequently denounced as 'secret'). He also claimed community in the 'sufferings which the two countries had received at the hands of the colonialists'. Relations thereafter were mildly coloured by inconspicuous economic and cultural exchanges. On the face of it the conclusion of a Sino-Afghan Treaty of Friendship and Mutual Non-Aggression in August 1960 represented a sudden advance to closer relations; and Marshal Chen Yi, signing it in Kabul, did not fail to bracket it with the agreements reached with Burma and Nepal as 'good examples of the implementation of the five principles of peaceful coexistence'. In a reference to Peking's advocacy of a nuclear-free zone in Asia he declared: 'The Chinese People's Republic has never committed and never will commit aggression against or injure others. On the contrary, China has up to now been subjected to aggression and injury by others.'

For Afghanistan the restrictive effects of a treaty of this kind were minimized by her existing relations with both the Soviet Union and the United States, and by the extremely small potential of her trade with China. The evident value of the treaty to China lay in the advertising, at India's expense, of a conciliatory Chinese attitude towards border-States; and an actual settlement of the strip of frontier-territory involved could therefore be postponed. When it was finally undertaken, and concluded in a boundary-treaty signed in Peking in November 1963, it could still be publicized in relation to the stalemate with India, and the Chinese Foreign Minister Chen Yi could offer his confidence 'that the Sino-Indian boundary-question would be fairly and reasonably settled in the end as China's boundary-questions with other south-western neighbours had been'. But the Chinese motive for delimitation at that stage may be thought to have been more closely connected with the encounter with the Soviets on the Sinkiang frontier than with the problem of India.

Pakistan was a different matter. There was the traditional claim of the Chinese Empire to the allegiance of Hunza, relating to a 150-mile border. It was this, as it later transpired, which clashed with the claims of the Pakistan Government, whose position was that Hunza had not in 1947 been a tributary of Kashmir and consequently remained unaffected by the Kashmir dispute with India.* There had been Chinese map-claims, one of which (September 1959) appeared to include some 6,000 square miles in the Hunza and Gilgit area as Chinese. There had been reports of Chinese military incursions (the first as early as April 1953), intrusions by Chinese aircraft and, after the Tibetan revolt in 1959, border-incidents and rumours of Chinese subversion. The tone of Chinese Communist comment on Pakistan, as a member of SEATO and a recipient of U.S. military aid, had been continuously hostile, and Peking had been sensitive to Pakistan's attitude and United Nations voting-record on matters relating to Taiwan and Tibet.

President Ayub Khan's statement that Pakistan was both willing to settle any frontier-problem with China and determined to resist intrusion was made on 23 October 1959. No overt response came from Peking during more than a year, and it was the Pakistani Foreign Minister who announced, on 15 January 1961, that he had received a Chinese acceptance 'in principle' of Pakistan's proposal that the frontier should be defined. The inconclusive meetings of Indian and Chinese officials for the docu-

---

* The much longer border of Baltistan, from Hunza eastwards to the Kashmir cease-fire line, which Peking wished to discuss with Pakistan and refused to discuss with India, was not at first regarded by Pakistan as appropriate for negotiation with China.

mentary examination of their problem had then just finished; and the refusal of the Chinese team to discuss any part of the frontier west of the Karakoram Pass (the Kashmir cease-fire line) had been a contentious issue. The Indian Government therefore asked the Pakistan Government, early in February, for a clarification of the reported agreement in principle for Sino-Pakistani frontier-definition.

The latent possibilities of exploiting tension between India and Pakistan to the Chinese advantage were being demonstrated. But with little incentive either for ideological détente with Pakistan or for removing frontier-doubts in the Pamir area, Peking allowed the matter to proceed by rumour and unconfirmed report. Not until 3 May 1962 did Peking announce officially that 'the Governments of China and Pakistan have agreed to negotiate on the boundary-question'. Both sides, it was added, had agreed that the resulting settlement would be provisional, pending a solution of the dispute over Kashmir between Pakistan and India. In this decision the fact that Soviet Russia was a declared supporter of India's case in the Kashmir argument doubtless played a part.

Five months later, just before the main Chinese assault across the McMahon Line, a further announcement stated that the talks with Pakistan had begun.

SIKKIM, BHUTAN AND THE 'FIVE FINGERS'
Circumstances had compelled the Chinese People's Government to treat with Nepal on terms of equal sovereignty, although it was on record that Mao Tse-tung before coming to power, had regarded it as a 'lost' Chinese property. It was also known that the term 'Five Fingers of Tibet', much used by the Chinese Communists in

subversive propaganda among the peoples of the Himalayan region, referred to Ladakh, Nepal, Sikkim, Bhutan and the Indian North-East Frontier Agency, as territories linked with Tibet and expected to share its destiny.

The Buddhists of Ladakh had a close cultural and historical relationship with Tibet, but if this were to sanction an extension of Chinese power it could only mean that Peking intended to push its demands on the 'unadministered' Aksai Chin down to the inhabited regions, including Leh itself. And at the same time, by the practice of treating their territorial claims in this area as part of Sinkiang, not of Tibet, and suggesting a Turki origin for place-names, the Chinese were presenting an entirely different 'cultural' argument. At the other extreme of the frontier-zone the aboriginal tribes of the Assam Himalaya offered a finger-touch with Tibet only near the borders of Bhutan, in the Tawang Tract. In the centre Nepal was customarily regarded, by the cultural test, as being in the Indian, rather than the Tibetan picture. There remained Sikkim and Bhutan, both of them south of the watershed, each of them linked with India, in the new period of Asian nationalities, by a treaty leaving the ultimate responsibility for external and frontier-relations in Indian hands.

On 8 September 1959, in the letter to Nehru which made the Chinese territorial demands official, Chou En-lai wrote:

In Your Excellency's letter, you also referred to the boundary between China and Sikkim. Like the boundary between China and Bhutan, this question does not fall within the scope of our present discussion. I would like, however, to take this opportunity to make clear once again that China is willing to live together in friendship with Sikkim and Bhutan, without committing aggression against each other, and has always respected the proper relations between them and India.

In the context this could only mean that the existing relations between India and Sikkim and Bhutan respectively were not recognized by the Chinese Government as 'proper'. The Chinese refusal to discuss with India the Sikkim and Bhutan sections of the boundary remained unshakeable. It thus appeared that in the view of Peking the two Hill-States were regarded either as competent to conclude treaties or else as subject in some way to China. The former status was denied if their treaty-relationships with India were ignored. The implication, in Gangtok and Paro as well as in Delhi, was obvious and sinister.

The position to be secured by dealing directly with Gangtok and Paro was certainly of more importance to the Chinese than a question of boundary-alignments. In the case of Sikkim the well established nature of its northern and eastern frontier was in itself a Chinese asset, since it resulted from a rare instance of bilateral Anglo-Chinese agreement on a portion of the Tibetan frontier (this frontier-article of the 1890 Anglo-Chinese Convention was confirmed between Britain and Tibet in 1904, repeated in the 1906 Anglo-Chinese Convention, and again confirmed with Tibet at Simla in 1914). The Chinese People's Government was therefore content to inform the Indian Government on 26 December 1959 that 'the boundary between China and Sikkim has long been formally delimited and there is neither any discrepancy between the maps, nor any dispute in practice'.

In the case of Bhutan also, though its much longer northern boundary had only a natural and traditional, not a treaty-based justification, Peking showed a tendency to play down the frontier-aspect of what it posed as a matter of relationship. Chinese map-claims had in fact sliced off a not inconsiderable area of eastern Bhutan, and in

October 1958 the Maharajah's Government had addressed Peking on this subject through the accepted Indian channel. Instead of acknowledging the protest by the same route, the Chinese contrived to convey covert suggestions within Bhutan to establish a direct correspondence with the Maharajah, but these were both rejected and revealed to the Indian Government. The Bhutanese boundary-question itself, which may have been raised chiefly as a means of pressure for direct discussions, was minimized in the Chinese note to India of 26 December 1959: 'Concerning the boundary between China and Bhutan there is only a certain discrepancy between the delineation on the maps of the two sides in the sector south of the so-called McMahon Line. But it has always been tranquil along the border between the two countries.'

But the location of this 'discrepancy' was significant, for it referred to Bhutan's eastern border with the Indian North-East Frontier Agency, not to the northern border with Tibet. It could not have come into question without an assumption of Chinese sovereignty to a depth of nearly 100 miles south of the McMahon Line. And it could not have been examined or demarcated without the physical possession which, in the NEFA invasion of October 1962, the Chinese appeared to be attempting by force of arms.

By that time Chinese maps had been amended, claims on Bhutan being dropped while those upon India had been retained or even increased. A further attempt to detach Bhutan by a display of partiality could be deduced from the Chinese care to avoid any trespass on the State, even in the area of their previous claim, in the thrust to the foothills made in close proximity to the Bhutanese border.

VIII

THE POLITICS OF INVASION
AND WITHDRAWAL

THE UNDECLARED WAR WITH INDIA

THE action taken by the Chinese towards the end of
October 1962, when purposeful military offensives were
mounted simultaneously in the western and eastern sectors of the Indian frontier, was of a scale and character so
far unique in Communist China's handling of boundary-
questions. It thus pointed the Chinese argument, developed during the preceding campaign to isolate India
politically, that India had transgressed the norms of
neighbourly relationship with the new China and of Afro-
Asian solidarity in face of the 'common enemy' identified
as Western imperialism. By the same token the Indian
reaction to the differential in the Chinese application of
boundary-principles was increased by the massive attempt
to force the issue in India's case alone. The point at which
'invasion' was substituted for 'intrusions' was instantly
recognizable. The fervour of national resistance was so
spontaneous as almost to embarrass the Indian Government. Abroad, despite the general and acute preoccupation with the Caribbean crisis, the recognition of a
turning-point in Asia was also immediate. The offer,
acceptance and implementation of Western military
assistance to India, though it must certainly have been
foreseen by the Chinese, may indeed have taken place
more quickly than they had calculated.

Neither invader nor invaded declared war, however,

although a state of emergency was declared by the President of India on 26 October (and by the Sikkim Government on 13 November). But diplomatic relations were not broken off. In an important respect the conflict remained limited in that both sides, for different reasons, avoided committing their air forces in an offensive capacity. And as early as 5 November, when the Chinese Government was awaiting with unconcealed impatience a 'positive response' from India to its three-point statement carried with the attack, the *Times of India* was shrewdly forecasting that 'a withdrawal when it is least expected would be characteristic of the manner in which the Chinese conduct their affairs'.

In the event the Chinese issued late on 20 November their unilateral declaration of a cease-fire as from midnight, to be followed by withdrawal of their forces, as from 1 December, to the 'line of actual control'. This was explained as meaning, in the eastern sector, the McMahon Line, and in the western sector the position as at 7 November 1959, when Chou En-lai had first put forward, after the Kongka Pass engagement in Ladakh, his proposal for a twenty-kilometre withdrawal by both sides in both sectors.

A number of factors played their part in the timing of this declaration. In determining the point at which it would become expedient, or feasible, to disengage themselves the Chinese had clearly something less than the military and political initiative with which they had opened the offensive. Invasion and withdrawal have nevertheless to be considered as a single instrument with a previously calculated use. The combined tactic had served the Manchus on different occasions, for example in Ladakh and in Nepal. The circumstances in which it had now to be operated were vastly different, involving political calculations of a new kind and on a widely international scale. The fixity of purpose within this complexity can be considered by examining, in the first place, what the Chinese announcement of a cease-fire and withdrawal expressly proposed in relation to the boundary-question. It was to require, as had previous Chinese statements on the subject, a good deal of 'clarification'. What was explicit, however, was the date of 7 November 1959. On the face of it, and since India was concerned at this stage simply to nullify the effects of the invasion by a restoration of the position (8 September 1962) before it took place, the climax might have appeared to be withdrawing further than necessary—in which case, as an Indian spokesman pointed out (27 November) 'it should be quite easy for China to accept India's proposal'. In fact, however, the position on the ground which the Chinese had aimed to rectify by invasion and withdrawal was one which, in Ladakh, had been changed in India's favour during the previous months.

For India this had been, quite literally, an uphill task. But by the summer of 1962 the newly established Indian defence-posts were in some cases behind the positions to which the Chinese had advanced. 'Some apprehension', suggested Nehru in parliament on 20 June, had thereby 'been created in the minds of the Chinese, and they have also moved'. Peking had added strong protests to its warnings that it would be 'dangerous for India to alter the *status quo* unilaterally'. Delhi, disturbed especially by the difficulty of discovering the limits, if any, of China's territorial ambitions in this sector, had adopted the 'vacation of aggression' (since 1957) as a condition for fruitful negotiations. This did not, however, imply an Indian aim of pushing forward into such vacated territory. Nehru's own 1959 proposal for a 'no-man's-land' in the Aksai Chin, though it had been rejected by the Chinese, still stood, and had been repeated on 14 May 1962, with the additional offer that, pending a negotiated settlement, the Chinese should be allowed the use of their Aksai Chin road for civilian traffic.

This was no doubt the most that an Indian Government responsible to public opinion could have offered at that stage. But it was plainly unacceptable to Peking: not because of the limitation to civilian use, which it would have been easy to circumvent, but because of its permissive form. It was in any case no moment for the Chinese to put their vital communications at risk. Trouble on the Sinkiang-Soviet border, with Chinese Kazakh subjects crossing in numbers into the USSR, reached critical proportions in the summer of 1962. Though the new posts established in Ladakh by the Indians did not constitute, from the Chinese side, a threat to the Sinkiang–Tibet road requiring massive preventive action there and elsewhere, India's negotiating position was at all events being improved, and with no little air of defiance. It was in the Ladakh sector that on 21 July shots were exchanged, for the first time anywhere along the frontier-zone since October 1959. More were to be expected, and at one point Nehru warned the Chinese Ambassador that there was a danger of drifting into war.

The situation reached in Ladakh in 1962, however, does not by itself explain the Chinese insistence, when the time came to operate withdrawal after invasion, on a 'line of actual control' dated at 7 November 1959. It could have been dated to the summer of 1961, when for the first time the strengthening of Indian positions took them, according to Chinese complaints, across the Chinese claim-line (some 100 miles within the map-frontier of Ladakh as understood by India.) The choice of 7 November 1959 was basic to Chinese policy in the following ways:

(1) Though not ill-content that vague or contradictory Chinese maps should keep India in some uncertainty as to their final claims, the Chinese Government had, by Chou En-lai's letter of 7 November 1959, taken their stand on the principle of effectively maintaining the *status quo* pending a settlement. This *status quo* was equated with 'the so-called McMahon Line' in the east and a 'line of actual control' in the west—the central sector, despite known points of dispute, being regarded as offering no serious obstacles to negotiation.

(2) By insisting that the entire length of the Sino-Indian frontier was undelimited, the Chinese proposed to exclude from effective consideration any treaties or boundary-agreements belonging to the past. The question was to be one of a 'traditional customary line', the location of which was in dispute between the two countries. On this showing, the very wideness of the dispute in the western and eastern sectors allowed no field for normal discussion. In the west, therefore, where the Chinese had advanced in a military sense to something approximating to the line they intended to claim, the 'line of actual control' and the 'traditional customary line' were gradually made into convertible terms. The *status quo* was the only basis for negotiation, and it must not be 'unilaterally altered by force'. In the east, though the *status quo* should be maintained pending negotiation, it was *not* to be the basis. The 'traditional customary line' of the Chinese claim was to be 100 miles south of the watershed, and unsupported at present by the factor of Chinese occupation.

(3) Nevertheless the letter of 7 November 1959 proposed, and subsequent communications maintained, that the same treatment of joint twenty-kilometres withdrawal should apply to both sectors. The pressure of Chinese occupation in the west, and of a magnanimous but menacing self-restraint in the east, must be simultaneously applied. The force of both would stand to be reduced by any serious documentary examination of what Nehru called 'the facts

in regard to the Sino-Indian boundary', which must therefore be resisted.

(4) Documentary examination in fact took place, in joint official sessions between June and December 1960. Inevitably they revealed no grounds of agreement. Inevitably, also, they produced considerably better evidence and argument for the Indian than for the Chinese case. The Indian Government, which stood to gain in terms of national unity and a sympathetic international hearing, published the joint Reports, both Indian and Chinese, at once (February 1961). The Chinese avoided the issue until April 1962, when repeated Indian references compelled a publication by Peking, though with external publicity confined to a brief and one-sided summary. The Chinese use of 7 November 1959 as the reference-point in the border-dispute thus served the further purpose of ignoring this development.

(5) The essential Chinese case was not legalistic but political, and it was not elaborated until November 1962, at a time and in circumstances of China's choosing. Its open endeavour, for the persuasion of the leaders of 'non-aligned' Afro-Asian countries addressed by Chou En-lai on 15 November, was to carry the imputation of Indian responsibility for the conflict as far back as possible. The concept of a peaceful *status quo* existing on 7 November 1959 supplemented this argument. To have found it at an even earlier date would have invalidated both the Chinese advance in Ladakh and their official claim south of the McMahon Line.

TIMING AND OBJECTIVES

The coincidence of the undeclared Sino-Indian frontier-war with the dangerous Russo-American clash over Cuba had an obvious consequence in restraining Soviet criticism of the Chinese action.* It cannot be concluded, however, that the Chinese offensive was specifically timed to take advantage of the Soviet involvement. The preliminary

* The Chinese three-point statement of 24 October was endorsed on the following day by *Pravda* and *Izvestia* as 'acceptable, constructive and sincere'. By 5 November, when the Cuba crisis was over, this endorsement had been dropped, although Moscow still avoided taking sides in the conflict between China and India.

Chinese moves in the Tawang area, near the Bhutan-India-China trijunction at the western end of the McMahon Line, had been made in early September. Seasonal limitations on movement, especially in Ladakh where light tanks as well as artillery were to be used, dictated that a major offensive must be developed by the end of October or be delayed for another year. While the strengthening of Indian positions within Ladakh seemed to the Chinese to call for a major counter-operation, an Indian proposal (26 July) for renewing boundary-discussions had taken its stand on the Nehru-Chou communiqué of 1960 and the Report of the joint examining officials which resulted from it. This had revived the prospect, unacceptable to Peking, of treating boundary-questions on their merits and thus isolating the Ladakh problem not only from that of the McMahon Line but from the general, and political, objectives pursued by the Chinese.

In other words, the credibility of the deterrent represented by the large Chinese claim in the eastern sector had been weakened. This political weapon had been patiently built up from nothing, in the sense that from 1950 to 1959 India's recognition of the McMahon Line as her boundary from Bhutan to Burma had gone unchallenged. The Chinese intention to use it as a means of pressure had been unconcealed since April 1960, when Chou En-lai's disposition to bargain as between the eastern and western sectors had been headed off by Nehru's demand for factual investigations. Chinese 'forbearance' in keeping to their own side of the McMahon Line (and eventually withdrawing, at Nehru's request, from the post they had overrun at Longju) had been a working component of the instrument. But if their territorial claims south of the Line were successfully ignored, or worse still, re-submitted to exposure by evidence, 'forbearance' would have ceased to function. This would be the point for reactivating the deterrent by invasion and withdrawal, and the form of the Indian proposal of July suggested that it had been reached. The call for talks 'as contemplated' in the 1960 Prime Ministers' communiqué could not be dismissed. It was guardedly approved by Peking on 4 August, with an accompanying demand that 'the Indian side stop advancing into Chinese territory'. Decisive action was then initiated to redress the political balance in the Chinese favour.

Whatever military considerations may have been embodied in the plan for two main thrusts in the eastern sector, there were political implications in the selection of the Tawang area at one end of the McMahon Line and the Walong area, 500 miles to the east, at the other. In both these areas there was a localized history of past claims on the part of Tibet and/or China, so that to that extent a mainly very reasonable Indian boundary was vulnerable.* At the eastern extremity, moreover, where the adjoining, and accepted, McMahon Line boundary between China and Burma had been left open 'pending a settlement' with India, the Chinese may have had special reasons for impressing the Lohit tribesmen with a show of mastery. At the western extremity, close to Bhutan, such a demonstration would certainly fall into the pattern of Chinese pressure upon the Hill-peoples. Every oppor-

* In *The China-India Border* (Chatham House, 1964) Dr Lamb suggests that, on a proper approach to the British before 1947, the Chinese could have legitimately expected some rectification of the McMahon Line at these points. They did not, he adds, seriously maintain that the 32,000 square miles of the wholesale claim down to the 'outer line' had ever, in fact, been Chinese, or even Tibetan. (This is what Chou En-lai did maintain, whether seriously or not, in his letter to Nehru of 8 September 1959.)

tunity of exerting such pressure was in fact taken by the Chinese during their advance, and at their withdrawal they left notices asserting their ability to return at will.

In the unlikely event of a swift Indian capitulation on the three points communicated by Chou En-lai to Nehru on the fourth day of the invasion (24 October), China would thus have had a *status quo* case for a 'rectified' line in the eastern sector as basis for the overall twenty-kilometre withdrawal which continued to represent the Chinese condition for frontier-negotiation. Three days later, with no Indian reply except a Presidential declaration of national emergency, Peking used the semi-official agency of the *People's Daily* for the most outspoken ideological attack yet made upon the Indian Prime Minister and Government; and from this article certain further Chinese objectives could be deduced, although at this stage they may have been no more than tentative. The article, for example, expressed concern for the overburdened people of India, now to be additionally loaded with heavy military expenditure—which might be taken as a hint that the Chinese were calculating upon a setback to India's economic development at a time of crisis in their own. There was also a call for political allies within India, and a reminder to Indian Communists and 'progressives' of many kinds that there were times when nationalist impulses should be subordinated to a wider and worthier cause.

THE ISOLATION OF INDIA

The title of this widely broadcast *People's Daily* article of 27 October—*More on Nehru's Philosophy in the Light of the Sino-Indian Boundary Question*—explicitly linked it with the earlier examinations of Nehru's ideology in relation to the Tibetan crisis, published by Peking in May 1959. And 'the root cause and background of the Sino-Indian boundary dispute' was now roundly said to be that 'in the effort to satisfy their own needs and the demands of U.S. imperialism, Indian ruling circles, headed by Nehru, have become pawns in the international anti-China campaign'. The Marxist approach was for once unconcealed, the Indian menace being said to arise from 'the inherent class-nature of the big bourgeoisie and big landlords of India, represented by Nehru, who are closely combined with imperialism'. There was much, indeed, to relate the argument (and with it the Chinese tactics towards India) to the current phase of the Communist ideological dispute, with Peking demonstrating a dynamic attitude in the anti-imperialist struggle and expressly refuting a recently publicized suggestion that Moscow had been exercising an effective and salutary restraint upon Chinese belligerence. There was also a particular line for the Hill States in a denunciation of India's posture as a protecting power, and for India's neighbours in general a picture of Nehru's ambition to establish 'a great empire unprecedented in India's history, the sphere of influence of which would far surpass that of the colonial system formerly set up in Asia by the British Empire'.

With new exaggerations Chinese propaganda at this definitive point was thus relying heavily on the theme of its long preliminary campaign to isolate India, its present Government in particular, and its Prime Minister in person, who had in the recent past been criticized for accepting aid from the United States, for failing at certain points to denounce U.S. imperialism, and for failing at others to applaud Soviet atom-tests. The image that had been presented of an imperialist-minded and aggressive India could be, and was, put to use in transferring responsibility for aggression in October 1962 from China to India. But for two reasons this cannot be seen as its main purpose. In the first place, though Indian aggression might be cited as cover in a conventional way, it could obviously carry no serious conviction in face of the major operation envisaged by the Chinese. In the second place, it was no part of China's policy to appear as the victim of aggression by a powerful neighbour. That posture had been definitely relegated to the past. The Chinese isolation of India by diplomacy and propaganda was a process of reducing the stature, prestige and alliances of a neighbour to the scale required for an appropriate relationship, including a frontier-settlement, with the new China of the People's Government. It had been initiated when Indian reactions to the developments in Tibet provoked Peking to state the principles of such a relationship, only to encounter an Indian refusal to align her policy and attitudes with those of Communist China.

Aside from Peking's attempt to persuade Moscow that the Chinese quarrel with India was a response to provocation, ideologically justified and deserving of something more positive than Soviet neutrality, the field for the operation to isolate India was the political buffer-zone of new, more or less non-aligned Afro-Asian States. Since the nucleus had first appeared at Bandung in 1955, China had been endeavouring to set and keep this growing group upon a suitably 'anti-imperialist' course. By 1959 India's view of Tibet, of the frontier-question and of the scope of her own independence, had marked her as off-course, but her prestige in the Afro-Asian group was high. The Belgrade 'non-aligned summit' meeting of September 1961 provoked Peking to distort Nehru's speeches, as well as his Government's policy, in a final, and partly success-ful attempt to reduce India's standing in this group of nations. Even her title to membership was impugned, and in the conflict of November 1962 Peking's presentation of India as an Afro-Asian renegade was used as much to remind other Governments of the obligations of 'the Bandung spirit', good-neighbourship with China and participation in the anti-imperialist struggle, as to confirm India's transgression of all three. It was this which was to be read in the prepared statement on the Sino Indian boundary-question issued on 16 November 1962, in the form of a letter from Chou En-lai addressed in individual copies to the Heads of State in non-aligned Asian and African countries. The case was furnished with a con-siderable number of maps, but gave only minor attention to any factual aspects of a disputed boundary. The dis-tinction of India from other States, such as Burma and Nepal, which had accepted frontier-settlements with China 'in the Bandung spirit' was not only placed first, but given as the reason for the Chinese Prime Minister's review of 'the background of the Sino-Indian boundary question'. This was then presented as a simple 'legacy of British Imperialist aggression', with the independent Indian Government as a willing legatee harbouring further 'covetous desires towards the Tibet region of China'. The conduct expected of a newly emerging Asian nation had been belied in the exhibition of 'a dark side to Sino-Indian relations from the very beginning'. This was traced from the Indian protest to Peking in 1950 (an attempt to 'obstruct the peaceful liberation of Tibet') to the wilful engineering of a border-dispute which had now culmin-ated in a frenzied military adventure resolutely dealt with

by the Chinese. The Afro-Asian Governments addressed
could be expected to appreciate the situation and support
Chinese endeavours towards a peaceful settlement, since
'almost unanimously they hold that the arch enemy of us
Asian and African countries is imperialism and colonialism'. And the kind of settlement indicated, to be achieved
by direct negotiation, was urged as essential in order 'to
cope with the main enemy'.

The emphasis on direct negotiations at the end of Chou
En-lai's letter was a warning that the Chinese Government would resist any idea of outside mediation in the
dispute such as President Nasser of the UAR, for one,
was thought to be contemplating. What China was suggesting was the pattern of Afro-Asian pressure that should
be exerted upon the Indian Government to accept, as it
had not yet done under invasion, Chinese proposals which
would have left the gains of invasion in the western sector
in Chinese hands. The first responses from Afro-Asian
Governments, though doubtless less favourable to India
than Delhi might have hoped, were less than satisfactory
to Peking. This may have had some influence on the
Chinese decision to complete the tactical process with the
declaration of a cease-fire and withdrawal on the night of
20 November. The next Afro-Asian move followed on
26 November, when the Ceylon Government proposed to
call a conference to consider the dispute between India
and China and to suggest steps for relieving tension. And
from 10 to 12 December representatives of the six non-
aligned States of Ceylon, Cambodia, Burma, Indonesia,
the UAR and Ghana conferred in Colombo.

There was no suggestion of mediation as an aim of the

Colombo Conference. Indian, as well as Chinese, opinion would have opposed the idea. But Nehru had told parliament on 10 December that the Indian Government would be prepared to refer the border-dispute to the International Court of Justice, provided the Chinese vacated their recent gains in Ladakh by withdrawing to the positions of 8 September 1962. China, in short, had failed to secure Indian acceptance of the basic demands first made, in the Indian phrase, 'at pistol-point' on 24 October, and essentially reiterated thereafter with varying forms of pressure. The effect of withdrawal itself was being reduced by the Indian Government's failure to accept its accompanying terms, while observing the cease-fire in practice and leaving the Chinese retirement unimpeded. To this Peking could only react by reserving 'the right to strike back'.

Before being published, the proposals of the Colombo Conference were explained to the Chinese and Indian Governments by a delegation to the two capitals. As revealed on 20 January 1963, the proposals represented a compromise between the Chinese and Indian positions regarding the terms for an extended cease-fire and for the opening of preliminary talks. In the eastern sector it was suggested that on the Chinese withdrawal behind the McMahon Line the Indian forces should be allowed to advance up to it, except at the two points where the location of the Line itself was in dispute. Since the central sector had not been affected in the fighting, the existing position should continue. In the western sector the proposals adopted for 'the line of actual control' the Chinese dateline of 7 November 1959, rather than the Indian dateline of 8 September 1962. But though a Chinese withdrawal of twenty kilometres behind this alignment was accepted, the Indians were to remain, militarily-speaking, in their 1959 positions. This would mean that most of the forty-three Indian defence-posts overrun by the Chinese offensive could not be re-activated. But in the de-militarized zone created between the armed forces of both sides, both could establish administrative civilian posts.

Before the publication of the Colombo proposals, Peking had described its response to them as a 'positive' one. A statement by Chen Yi on 21 January, however, revealed that the Chinese Government had certain reservations. The Indian Government's acceptance of the proposals 'in principle', which had been previously communicated (13 January) to Ceylon as convener of the Colombo Conference, became on 26 January, after a three-day debate in both Houses of the Indian Parliament, an acceptance *'in toto'*. On 2 March the Chinese Government informed the Indian Government that their withdrawal plans had been completed, in terms deliberately implementing their own declaration ('20 kilometres from the line of actual control as of 7 November 1959, along the entire Sino-Indian border'). Their attitude to the Colombo proposals did not move, then or later, from 'positive response' and 'acceptance in principle'. Resuming his correspondence with Nehru on 3 March, Chou En-lai made it clear that:

(i) 'In order to promote direct Sino-Indian negotiations the Chinese Government has done all that is possible for it to do.'

(ii) The Chinese insistence on direct negotiations 'will not change'. A settlement, he added on 20 April, could only be reached thus and 'absolutely not through any form of arbitration'.

(iii) Such direct negotiations could and should begin at once.

The Chinese Government maintained its reservations on the Colombo proposals, but did not regard this as a reason for postponing negotiation.

It was at the same time evident from Chou En-lai's letter that the existing stalemate—'a *de facto* cease-fire and a *de facto* disengagement along our border' produced by 'the initiative and efforts of the Chinese side'—was something with which the Chinese might be prepared to live indefinitely. China would be patient, appreciating that the Indian Government, 'owing to the needs of its internal and external politics', might find it difficult to negotiate at once. This was doubtless to be understood as a hint that Indian policy was compromised by the compulsion to accept Western military assistance. As such it must have recalled the Chinese note of 1950 which attributed Indian representations on the Chinese Army's move into Tibet to 'foreign influences hostile to China'. It was equally repudiated.

The specific reservations on the Colombo proposals in which the Chinese Government persisted were substantial. Their objections were to an Indian military return to the McMahon Line itself (apart from the disputed localities of Thagla and Longju); and to the sanction for Indian civilian posts in the proposed zone of demilitarization in Ladakh. From the Indian viewpoint, it was only the provision for this limited Indian presence that could justify even a temporary acquiescence in the territorial position brought about by the Chinese invasion. The Chinese appeared equally determined to retain some result from their large-scale operation. In the western sector they accordingly proceeded to establish their own administrative posts, as of right, in what would have been the demilitarized zone, while denying any Indian title to do so 'on Chinese territory'.* And in the eastern sector the absence of such Chinese posts in the areas of localized dispute was once more represented as a gesture of forbearance.

But the significance of the Chinese reservations, retained while assuming that negotiations could proceed, was wider. It meant that, even if Peking had concessions to bring to the negotiating-table, negotiations must be opened in terms of a powerful Chinese demand, not in terms of a compromise evolved by other parties. Since the Indian Government's determination not to place itself in this relationship did not weaken, considerations of the possibilities open to boundary-adjustment remained irrelevant. The resultant stalemate continued to be virtually unbroken, though there was a fairly steady flow of protest and counter-protest on the alleged treatment of each party's nationals, on local intrusions and a variety of contentious incidents. The Indian Government, taking its stand on the Colombo proposals, was in a position to keep the light of attention playing upon Chinese intransigence in face of the unanimous view of six non-aligned Afro-Asian States. The Chinese expressed Indian intransigence in the charge that Delhi was insisting on a 'precondition' (Chinese acceptance of the Colombo proposals) for peaceful negotiations.

OTHER CHINESE SETTLEMENTS

There were good reasons why a prolonged stalemate on the Indian border should commend itself to the Chinese

* Nehru eventually stated that India would be prepared to forgo the Colombo provision for interim civilian check-posts in the demilitarized zone of Ladakh, and to enter on this basis into negotiations, provided Chinese posts were withdrawn. On 22 May 1964 he said there had been no reaction from Peking to this offer.

after their invasion and withdrawal. What their tactics had gained was the removal of the Indian military posts on the edge of the strategically important Chinese claim in Ladakh; a demonstration of Chinese offensive strength with a consequent diminution of India's power-status; and a menacing advantage in the campaign to over-shadow the Himalayan peoples and to draw Sikkim and Bhutan into a direct and subservient contact. An unsettled *status quo* offered better prospects of consolidating these gains than any settlement that might be arrived at on the basis of the Colombo proposals. What they had failed to gain was Indian submission to the negotiating conditions which invasion and withdrawal had been intended to enforce; and this failure would be the more exposed if negotiations were to be opened as envisaged by the Colombo Conference. The inevitable build-up of Indian military capacity with Western assistance was unlikely, in the absence of further Chinese provocation, to produce a direct danger to the Chinese position for some considerable time. Simultaneously it tended to preclude any opportunity for a repetition of the kind of operation mounted by the Chinese in October 1962. In conditions of stalemate, however, there might be side-effects of some advantage to the Chinese: substantiation for the Peking propaganda aligning India with the 'imperialists'; an unsettling, anti-climactic effect upon Indian public opinion; and a damaging diversion of Indian resources to defence.

A point of political difficulty was the involvement of China in a policy of defiance of the six Colombo Afro-Asian States. Here, again, the best hope of emerging from the entanglement might be seen to lie in a long period without an obvious frontier-crisis, with India being slowly manœuvred into the rôle of a saboteur of Asian tranquillity.

From July to October 1963 no policy-statements on the Indian boundary-question emerged from Peking. Early in October, however, there were evident signs that the Governments of the UAR, Ceylon and Ghana were considering the convening of a further meeting of the Colombo Conference States to probe the possibilities of breaking the Sino-Indian deadlock. Peking's desire to forestall this could be seen, between 9 and 13 October, in a Chinese Government note to India, an interview given by Chou En-lai to a *Reuter* correspondent, and a *People's Daily* editorial suggesting that there was no great urgency in the matter. 'The question will eventually be settled peacefully, no matter how long it will take.'

In the meantime the picture of Communist China as a country eager for peaceful border-settlements with neighbours of any political complexion had been taken further by agreements with Pakistan, Afghanistan and the Mongolian People's Republic. All of these had some bearing, and the Mongolian settlement a special one, on the openly worsening state of Sino-Soviet relations. And the Chinese Communist Party's letter to the Soviet Party dated 29 February 1964 (released by Peking on 8 May in a batch of seven Sino-Soviet exchanges), presented India and the Soviet Union in bracketed hostility as the only two countries which had failed to settle with China the complicated boundary-questions left over from the past. All three agreements were also strongly exploited for the improvement of China's image among the Afro-Asian peoples.

At the end of 1962 the element of opportunism had been obvious in Peking's double announcement—on 26 December of a settlement 'in principle' of frontier-questions between China and Pakistan, and on the following day of the conclusion of a frontier-agreement between China and the Mongolian People's Republic. The recommendations of the Colombo Conference were not yet known, but Mrs Bandaranaike of Ceylon was due in Peking on 31 December to report them to the Chinese Government before undertaking a similar mission in Delhi. Afro-Asian opinion generally had welcomed the Chinese announcement of cease-fire and withdrawal rather than the proposed conditions for negotiation that accompanied it. The Chinese campaign to place India in 'the vanguard of imperialism' had reached a point of apparent desperation with the presentation of the Indian contribution to the United Nations force in the Congo as evidence for the charge. Only Laos, balancing the prospects of security as a small and exposed neighbour, had cabled 'very great satisfaction' to Chou En-lai and his Government. It was at this moment that Peking presented in the Sino-Mongolian settlement 'a good example of the handling of relations between Socialist countries'; and in the stage reached with Pakistan a further victory for the five principles of peaceful coexistence, adding weight to the contention that 'it is now time for the Indian Government to respond positively to China's peaceful proposals'.

The Mongolian agreement (which will be mentioned in the following chapter) was remarkably sudden in its appearance, only ten days after the first indication from Peking that the question had been taken up, or even that it existed. In the matter of Pakistan it was the acceleration that was striking. It had taken three years, after Pakistan's declaration that it was prepared to discuss frontier-questions, to bring the Chinese to begin them, on the eve of their action against India. Two months had then been enough to produce a settlement in principle, publicized by

Peking on the day that Indian and Pakistani officials were to open talks on the Kashmir problem, any solution of which would naturally reduce a considerable Chinese advantage. In no more than three months thereafter a Sino-Pakistan frontier-agreement was ready, to be signed in Peking on 2 March 1963.

India could have been expected to express concern over these proceedings, and did so. The legalistic contention that it was an Indian frontier that was being discussed with Pakistan could be answered, however, by the under-standing already expressed that a Sino-Pakistani settle-ment would be regarded by both parties as provisional, pending a solution of the Kashmir dispute between India and Pakistan. Indian protests could thus serve the Chinese, not only to maintain or increase Indo-Pakistani tension, but to emphasize the alleged Indian opposition to the peaceful settlement of frontier-disputes.

The essential justification of Indian resentment lay rather in the renewed demonstration that the Chinese were prepared, in boundary-discussions with other countries, to adopt methods and principles which they were unwilling to apply to the Indian question. The acceptance of a traditional and customary boundary-line, characterized by natural features, had been evident in the settlements with Burma and Nepal and was stated in Article 1 of China's agreement with Pakistan. It could further be noted that maps of the large scale (1 : 1 million) which the Chinese had been unable or unwilling to provide for their boundary-examinations with Indian officials in 1960, were used by both parties in the Sino-Pakistani talks.

The exact territorial results of the agreement with Pakistan were, and are, more difficult to assess. And it was here that Indian press-reactions tended to weaken the broad charge of deliberate Chinese partiality towards neighbours other than India. Various estimates, all of them indignant, of the extent of 'Indian territory given to China by Pakistan', would encourage the conclusion that large Chinese demands need not, after all, preclude a peaceful settlement. These estimates, however, were evidently at fault. It is more correct to see the agreement with Pakistan as a further instance of a Chinese readiness to waive or reduce a territorial claim (in some cases exaggerated in advance) where the solution of a boundary-problem becomes politically expedient.

The first estimates published in Karachi at the time of the agreement offered the following figures:

Area in previous dispute:	3,400 square miles
Agreed as China's territory (Shaksgam-Muztagh Valley area):	2,050 square miles
Agreed as Pakistan's territory (including 750 square miles which had been under Chinese control)	1,350 square miles

The state of previous national proprietorship east of the Pamir trijunction and among and beyond the high glaciers of the Karakoram, however, was neither simple nor stable. For twenty years after the Anglo-Russian Convention of 1907 (which was in prospect of revision when the Russian Revolution of 1917 closed the matter) the situation was linked with the claims of the Mir of Hunza to outlying grazing-grounds and other territory north of the understood watershed. Different forward alignments, advanced even beyond the Yarkand River in Sinkiang, had been considered and had appeared on

British maps. By 1927 they had (like the Mir himself) disappeared from serious policy, though not yet from the maps. With the emergence of independent India and Pakistan, Indian maps withdrew the northern boundary of Kashmir to something much more like a main watershed line (the Ladakh salient in the east of Kashmir was, of course, independent of the Karakoram range as a boundary-feature). But the first Pakistan maps did not show this considerable rectification.*

The Chinese Communist claim in their 1960 map (the map which increased their previous official demands in Ladakh) thus represented a very much deeper bite into Kashmir by reference to the outdated and abandoned British alignments than by reference to the frontier as officially accepted by India in all maps submitted in her dispute with the Chinese. The Chinese policy of refusing to include this part of the frontier in the exchange of evidence with India contributed, no doubt, to the persistence of confusion. But in the final analysis it seems true to say that in their settlement with Pakistan the Chinese, though advancing in the Muztagh Valley beyond the frontier as it had actually existed, did in fact abandon more of their published claims than they retained. They must also be held to have implicitly relinquished their traditional assumption of suzerainty over Hunza. Moreover, while proclaiming an Indian hostility to China, in alignment with the Western Powers, as 'the root cause of the Sino-Indian dispute', they had swiftly and smoothly come to terms with an Asian member of SEATO and CENTO.

On the same day as the Sino-Pakistan agreement (2

* The elucidation of this question is derived in part from Dr Alistair Lamb's *The China-India Border* (Chatham House, 1964).

March 1963) it was announced by the Chinese and Afghan Governments that their common border would be delimited in the near future. The sequence appeared logical: and no less so, perhaps, the definitive *People's Daily* article that followed within a week (8 March), bringing to open attention the existence of long-standing territorial questions between Communist China and the USSR. The Sino-Afghan boundary, less than fifty miles long but regarded by Peking as a contentious subject down to 1953, presented no difficulties. In June 1963 a small Chinese delegation arrived in Kabul. A preliminary delimitation was initialled almost at once (1 July), and a Sino-Afghan Boundary Treaty was signed in Peking on 22 November. Though the location of the trijunction still allowed a small margin of doubt (three miles or so) it was clear that a watershed frontier as existing in practice, though hitherto without a Chinese treaty-signature, had been accepted. In the summer of 1964 the final demarcation-procedures were given much publicity by Peking.

IX

SINO-SOVIET BORDER-TENSIONS

THE ILLUSION OF STABILITY

THE zone of power-contact which had provided the setting for Mao's protracted negotiations with Stalin in 1949–50 stretched from the High Pamir to the Gulf of Chih-li on China's Pacific coastline. It included the huge area of Outer Mongolia, in which the Soviet preponderance had insured itself by the (manifestly 'unequal') treaty with Chiang Kai-shek. It included also the Sino-Korean frontier-zone, where Stalin had had the advantage of supplying the Allied occupation-force for the northern part of Korea as well as the direction of Kim Il Sung's Workers' (Communist) Party. The initiative, at least, for the North Korean invasion of the southern Republic is presumed to have been Stalin's, and only after his death did the Chinese Communists enter warily upon a process of military disengagement in the peninsula.

It was only after Stalin's death, moreover, that the ambiguities of the Sino-Soviet accommodation gave some signs of being dispersed in the sensitive areas of Sinkiang and Manchuria. Soviet evacuation of Manchuria within three months of the defeat of Japan had been promised to the KMT Government in 1945, but not, of course, carried out. Under the 1950 Treaty with the People's Government Soviet special privileges in Manchuria, including the Port Arthur base, should have been relinquished in 1952, but they were then largely retained, ostensibly by Chinese 'invitation'. After the visit to Peking of Malenkov and Khrushchev (at that time second in command) in October 1954, the 1950 Treaty was adjusted and Soviet withdrawal took on tangible reality, in association with the grant of Soviet credits and economic and technical assistance. Agreement for joint Sino-Soviet economic enterprise in the frontier-zone of the Amur River followed in 1956. In the Central Asian area of contact the abolition in 1955 of the Joint Stock Companies set up in 1950 (for the exploitation of oil, minerals and other resources), appeared to mark the end of a long chapter in which Sinkiang had been virtually an economic province of Russia.

In none of these developments was there any public mention of frontier-questions. Despite the Chinese tendency to mark as 'undefined' or 'undelimited' frontiers which Soviet maps assumed to be firmly established, it thus appeared that the new relationship envisaged a prolonged acceptance of the *status quo*, or 'line of actual control'.

TROUBLE IN SINKIANG

In the Central Asian zone, more than in any other, the picture of 'actual control' was already being profoundly affected by the Chinese Communist determination to carry through a process of political, economic, ethnic and cultural colonization. Whether to secure the border or to subdue the Muslim inhabitants, the process had equally to be a military one. It seems probable that the Soviet 'Virgin Lands' campaign across the border in Kazakhstan (initiated in 1954) was in one aspect a counter to the Chinese programme. It is certain that the latter provoked resentment and serious disturbances inside Sinkiang, of

8. Central Asian Area

the kind of which Russian policy in the past had never failed to take advantage. When, and to what extent, Russian policy began to do so under the Khrushchev régime, is difficult to determine, since both Governments had the means and the will to suppress information. But it is at least curious that, according to the Soviet defector Alexandr Kaznacheev, the special department of the Soviet International Relations Institute which trained security-cadres for work in Sinkiang was never closed.*

Some suggestion of the scale of popular resistance to the Chinese establishment (September 1955) of the Sin-kiang-Uighur Autonomous Region can be derived from the figure of '90,000 remnant bandits' officially declared (March 1954) to have been wiped out by units of the North-West Military District of the People's Liberation Army. Soviet nationals had been gradually withdrawn across the border after 1954, but from 1958 (and possibly earlier) refugees from Sinkiang had been accepted with their herds in Soviet territory and re-settled. In that year Chinese sources referred to disorders provoked by 'counter-revolutionary and nationalist elements'. And in March 1959, when Sinkiang was reinfected by the revolt in Tibet, the problem of dissident peasants and herdsmen in the region of the Sino-Soviet border was referred to in the Sinkiang *Ili Daily*.

In May 1960 the Chinese Press carried descriptions of army life in the recently strengthened frontier defences of the Pamir plateau. In 1961 a Soviet report of the capture of spies 'coming from remote Sinkiang' appeared in *Kazakhstanskaya Pravda*. In the spring of 1962 the Chinese control of Sinkiang suffered fresh disturbances, which before the autumn seem to have amounted to serious revolt; and the reports and rumours which reached the outside world early in 1963 suggested that the Soviet Union was considerably involved. When frontier-relations

* 'Quite to the contrary,' wrote Kaznacheev in *Inside a Soviet Embassy* (1962), 'it was made even more efficient and staffed with even more strictly selected students. . . . The Sinkiang Department is working right now.'

became an open issue in the Sino-Soviet arguments of 1963–4, the detailed charges made by both sides confirmed that one of the centres of unrest had been Ining, capital of the Ili-Kazakh Autonomous Chou. The Chinese territorial grievance in the Ili frontier-region, announced on 8 March 1963 by the inclusion of the 1881 Treaty of St Petersburg (or of Ili) in the *People's Daily*'s list of 'unequal treaties', was historically the result of Russian exploitation of the Sinkiang rebellion of 1864, a century earlier.

BEHIND THE MONGOLIAN SETTLEMENT

This declaration of March 1963 concerning frontier-issues that could, if necessary, be raised with the Soviet Union at 'an appropriate time', referred to a special Chinese policy towards 'socialist' countries, though without defining it. If the sudden settlement of the Sino-Mongolian boundary a few months earlier (26 December) were to be considered as an example, fraternal agreements in the Communist world should be reached swiftly, after an exchange of unpublished communications: not by bringing contentious matters into the open with challenges of the sort that were to be flung between Moscow and Peking.

In so far as the Chinese agreement with the Mongolian People's Republic represented the conversion of an undetermined* into an established boundary, it could have been proceeded with at any time since the establishment of Mao Tse-tung's régime in 1949. But although details of the settlement are still unclear, it appears to have dealt with a number of territorial discrepancies, and to have

* Undetermined in Communist Chinese maps. Soviet maps, like most international atlases, showed a fixed frontier.

173

corrected them to the Mongolian advantage. The compensating political gains which were sought by Peking may no doubt be seen in the light of an attempt to save what could be saved from the long process of Chinese defeat in Outer Mongolia at the hands of Russia. A similar aim could have been seen in 1950, when Mao Tse-tung had to face the *fait accompli* of Outer Mongolian 'independence' wrested by Stalin from Chiang Kai-shek in 1945. By the terms of the Sino-Soviet Treaty Mao gained the somewhat fine point of recognizing the 'independent status', rather than the 'independence' of the Mongolian People's Republic, as well as the omission of any reference to an existing boundary with China such as Chiang Kai-shek had had to acknowledge. More practically, the Peking Government could and did benefit from the changed situation by establishing an embassy in Ulan Bator, where ineffective Chinese 'suzerainty' had not even been able to retain a representative. And from diplomatic and treaty-relations flowed cultural and economic agreements enabling Peking to compete with Moscow for influence over the wary Mongolians.

Although this competition was to make the Mongolian People's Republic the most heavily subsidized satellite, per head of population, in the Communist camp, Chinese offers of economic and technical assistance could inevitably be outbid by the greater Soviet resources. In the less material field of cultural influence based on common traditions, the Chinese might have held some advantage with the Mongolian element of their multi-racial State. As against this, the only people in the USSR belonging to the Mongol group by both race and language were the Buryat-Mongols in their small 'Autonomous Soviet Republic'. This possibility, however, is obviously compromised by the Communist ideology and Communist programmes. The existence of a Communist régime in Ulan Bator did not mask the fact that a similar régime in Peking was deliberately restricting, as 'local nationalism', the Mongol culture and language in Inner Mongolia. In 1950 the Mongols accounted for about one-third of the total population of the province. In 1954 the adjoining province of Suiyuan, with a predominantly Chinese population, was incorporated in Inner Mongolia, and Han migration continued the process of absorption. By 1962 Chinese outnumbered Mongols in the Inner Mongolian Autonomous Region by as much as ten to one. And in that year Mongol unrest in the region, which had been suppressed in 1949–54 with official casualties of 8,000 'bandits', again came to a head.

The eventuality prophesied by Mao Tse-tung in 1936, that 'the Outer Mongolian Republic will automatically become part of the Chinese federation of their own free will', had receded to vanishing-point. Soviet ascendancy, on the other hand, had been signalized in particular by the entry of the Mongolian People's Republic, under Soviet auspices, into the United Nations in 1961 (an event pointedly ignored in Chinese publicity); by its admission, in June 1962, as the only Asian member of the Soviet economic organization COMECON; and by its marked support of the Soviet line in the rift with Albania revealed at the 22nd CPSU Congress in November 1961. In this phase of the traditional Mongol policy of balance between two powerful neighbours, mistrust of Peking was evidently greater than mistrust of Moscow. A Chinese recognition of the frontier, on terms advantageous to the Mongolian People's Republic, ought to reduce that mistrust.

There is evidence that the Chinese were confident of improved relations in the fact that the Mongolian Prime Minister Tsedenbal was accorded a mass rally in Peking in which to express his appreciation when the frontier-agreement was signed. But his speech, though otherwise appropriate, included an unmistakable defence of Khrushchev against the Chinese attacks on the issue of the Cuba crisis. Thereafter the Mongolian loyalty to Moscow was confirmed with increasing candour, not only in the ideological aspect of the Sino-Soviet argument but in the clash of 'State relations' with its eventual reference to boundary-questions. By June 1964, the Mongolian Communist (People's Revolutionary) Party was prepared to acknowledge, in a Central Committee resolution, the deterioration of Sino-Mongolian relations as a consequence of Peking's fallacious principles and sinister policies, including 'racial discrimination, nationalism and big State chauvinism' towards 'national minorities, particularly Kazakhs, Uighurs and Inner Mongolians'. From the Chinese side, Mao himself was reported to have said, in an interview given to Japanese journalists on 10 July 1964, that the Soviet Union, 'under the pretext of guaranteeing the independence of Mongolia, actually placed that country under its domination'. This drew a sharp reply from the Mongolian Party newspaper *Unen*.

THE NORTH-EASTERN ZONE

The treaties brought into question by the Chinese on 8 March 1963 had evidently been chosen so as to equate territorial grievances against Russia (Aigun and Tientsin 1858, Peking 1860, Ili or St Petersburg 1881) with the questions of Hong Kong, Macao and Taiwan on which Khrushchev had taunted the Chinese with inaction (Nanking 1842, Lisbon Protocol 1887, Shimonosekei 1895, etc.). The revival, by reference to the Aigun and Peking Treaties, of Chinese claims in the north-east was for two reasons more striking than the note of dissatisfaction with the Sinkiang frontiers. In the first place, the Manchurian frontiers with the Soviet Far East were not a 'minority zone' but one in which there had been heavy Chinese settlement, so that it had not been subject to the disturbances endemic in the Sinkiang frontier-area. In the second place the Sino-Soviet programme of joint enterprise for the development of hydro-electric and other resources of the Amur-Ussuri basin had suggested that China's existing north-east frontiers were accepted by both sides. This development seemed to have been unaffected by the restriction of Soviet aid and the withdrawal of Soviet technicians from China; and Krushchev had in July 1962 reported it to COMECON (of which China was not a member) as an example of 'the further strengthening of economic ties between socialist countries'.

Isolated references, however, had shown that both sides had maintained a state of vigilance beyond what a 'frontier of peace' would seem to require. As a Soviet Far East official put it on 28 May 1960 (Soviet 'Border Guard Day'), the Amur and Ussuri boundaries 'now link two brotherly nations for ever, but Soviet Far Eastern border guards will never forget that enemies have always tried and will try to hamper Communist construction'. The life of these border guards, wrote a Soviet correspondent in the frontier-city of Blagoveshchensk in July, 1962, was 'tense but interesting', and even schoolchildren were recommended to be on the alert.

The historical process by which the Russian Empire acquired its Maritime Provinces in the Far East was too obviously predatory for the Soviet Government to deny. The most that it can do, as was shown in the long article published by *Pravda* on 4 September 1964, is to point out that the despoiled Chinese power was also an imperial one which happened to have got there first, and to claim that since the treaty-cessions to Russia 'the present border has developed historically and was fixed by life itself'. Whatever the line of argument, however, the Chinese can have no expectation of a voluntary Soviet surrender of an area of such importance, including the port of Vladivostok. As Mao Tse-tung was reported to have said to the Japanese journalists on 10 July 1964, 'we have not yet requested a settling of this account'. It is by keeping the account outstanding that the Chinese Communists can most effectively brand 'Soviet revisionism' as essentially imperialistic in character.

MATTERS OF PRINCIPLE

Agreement to hold talks on Sino-Soviet frontier-issues was indicated by Chou En-lai on 23 January 1964, and these began in Peking at embassy level on 25 February. On 8 May, when Peking released the full texts of a number of letters exchanged between the two Communist Parties from 29 November 1963 to 7 March 1964, the understanding on which the talks were being conducted was revealed. The Soviet letter of 29 November 1963 had said among other things:

Statements have recently been made in China concerning the aggressive policy of the Tsarist Government and the unjust treaties imposed upon China. Naturally we will not defend the Russian Tsars who permitted arbitrariness in laying down the State boundaries with neighbouring countries. We are convinced that you, too, do not intend to defend the Chinese Emperors who, by force of arms, seized not a few territories belonging to others. But . . .

historically-formed boundaries between States now exist. Any attempt to ignore this can become the source of misunderstandings and conflicts.

The Chinese reply of 29 February 1964 (four days after talks had started) showed that the position had been accepted, and that large Chinese territorial claims were not—or not yet—going to be pressed: 'Although the old treaties relating to the Sino-Russian boundary are unequal treaties, the Chinese Government is nevertheless willing to respect them and take them as the basis for a reasonable settlement.' It can be seen that the Soviet position—agreement to negotiate adjustments in an existing frontier but refusal to consider demands for 'large chunks of territory' —was similar to that adopted by the Indian Government but persistently rejected by Peking. The only difference was that India had supported the fact with treaty-evidence. The Soviet Government was prepared to disavow the evidence while insisting on the fact.

What progress, if any, was made in the Sino-Soviet negotiations was not revealed. But the political implications of the frontier-question were freely exploited by both sides. The very revival of Chinese territorial claims, in the *People's Daily* article of 8 March 1963, had been made in the context of the doctrinal schism, and in reference to the Soviet handling of the Caribbean crisis. And the chief question which the new argument illuminated was that of Chinese and Soviet rivalry for the control of the minority nationalities in Central Asia. In September 1963, while Moscow complained of 'systematic' Chinese violations of the border since 1960 (with more than 5,000 such intrusions in 1962 alone), Peking began to give its account of the 1962 events in Sinkiang: 'The leaders of the CPSU used their organs and personnel in Sinkiang,

China, to carry out huge-scale subversive activities in the Ili region and enticed and coerced several tens of thousands of Chinese citizens into going to the Soviet Union.' The Soviet side of the picture, most of it put out semi-officially with 'eye-witness accounts' from the Central Asian Republics of the USSR, gave a figure of 50,000 Chinese Muslim subjects taking refuge in Kazakhstan, Tadzikhistan and Kirghizia 'in the clothes they stood up in'. They had fled from 'the notorious Chinese agricultural communes which burst like soap-bubbles'. Attempting to stop the efflux, Chinese military forces in the Ili Kazakh Autonomous Chou had in May 1962 poured machine-gun fire into a large crowd applying for permits to leave. The Soviet Consul in Ining, though appealed to for arms and support for independence, was said to have refused to become involved. Despite this, the Chinese had closed down his consulate, as well as the other Soviet consulates in Tacheng and the Sinkiang capital, Urumchi.

On 11 October 1963 Chou En-lai told *Reuters* that these serious issues belonged to the past and 'the situation has recently become better'. There had been evidence, however, of similar disturbances, flights, and accusations of Soviet collusion during 1963, and Chinese charges were soon repeated. This occurred notably in the letter to the CPSU of 29 February 1964 in which the Chinese Communists had conceded that the 'old, unequal treaties' could nevertheless provide the basis of a frontier-settlement. The proviso that such a settlement could be reached only in an accommodating spirit and 'if the Soviet side takes the same attitude as the Chinese Government' required, apparently, that Soviet border-provocations, 'breaches of the *status quo*' and incitement of China's national minorities should be discontinued.

The purpose of Soviet propaganda on this issue, which was not discontinued, can be seen as twofold. There was the general disparagement of Chinese Communist policies openly connected with 'splitting activities' and 'racialism'. There was also an attempt to build up an argument for the existing frontier on the basis of Soviet benevolence towards the national minorities on her own side of it. To counter these effects, the Chinese stepped up their own propanganda-attention to developments in their minority regions, emphasizing material progress and general solidarity. But a concurrent campaign against 'the counter-revolutionary sabotage activities of the national minorities within our country' was launched in *Red Flag* on 30 June 1964. And it leaves no doubt that the pacification of its non-Chinese subjects is one of the major unsolved problems of the Chinese Communist régime.

Since the cherished 'union of nationalities' was a basic aim of Sun Yat-sen and the Chinese revolutionary revival, the failure to achieve it is an indictment of the Communist system. As such it must be, and is, laid at the door of others. And since the greater part of China's land-frontiers lie in zones which are the homeland of Tibetans, Kazakhs, Uighurs, Mongolians and other minorities, frontier-questions are vitally connected with those of national cohesion and central authority. This applies in particular to large stretches of the boundary with Soviet Russia, and the whole of the boundary with India. 'Among all our neighbours', said the Chinese Communist Party in its letter to the CPSU of 29 February 1964, 'it is only the leaders of the CPSU and the reactionary nationalists of India who have deliberately created border disputes with China.'

THE FRONTIERS OF CHINA

THE SOVIET AND THE INDIAN QUESTIONS

In bringing into question the vast and historic expansion of the Russian Empire into Asia, the Chinese Communists have made their picture of independent India as the heir of imperialism look even less realistic than it was. The Russian Maritime Provinces had originally been colonized by the Chinese, Chinese imperial authority had extended at different times beyond the present boundaries in the west, and Mongol and Manchu history gave Peking a somewhat better title to Outer Mongolia than it ever had to Tibet. Faced with preponderant power, however, and dealing with a 'socialist' ally, the Chinese were prepared to discuss border-questions on the basis of the Soviet position that 'only certain more accurate definitions of the frontier can be discussed where necessary'.*

It is likely that the original Soviet disinclination to support China's frontier-case against India in 1959 took into account the possible use of 'anti-imperialist' arguments against her own position in Asia. In the subsequent course of the Sino-Indian dispute the examination of evidence enlightened many people (including, perhaps, the Indian experts themselves) on a period of history in which the British imperial power had frequently been exercised for sustaining China against Russian expansion. And when Moscow at last moved, in September 1964, towards more definite support for the Indian case, it was manifestly as a warning to the Chinese not to promote a similar conflict with the USSR. A *Pravda* article of 19 September 1964 criticized Peking for avoiding the 'reasonable' Colombo proposals for talks with India, and found it 'difficult to believe in the sincerity of the Chinese

* Suslov's report to the CPSU Central Committee, 3 April 1964.

182

leaders, who give assurances that they are striving towards a peaceful settlement'. This was the Chinese sincerity that *Pravda* had urged India to accept when it had been offered in conjunction with military invasion.

Deadlock over the Colombo proposals produced no official Peking move to introduce new theoretical considerations into the dispute with India. But on 18 March 1963 a Chinese expert on international law, Chang Hung-tseng, contributed to the *Kwangming Daily* an article refuting the line of argument on 'natural frontiers' which had been much used by India in relation to the Himalayan watershed. Among Chou En-lai's 'Six Points' of April 1960, which had been considered important enough to be repeated in his letter to Afro-Asian leaders of 15 November 1962, 'certain geographical principles, such as watersheds, river-valleys and mountain-passes' had been accepted. But the point had been that they should apply equally to all sections of the boundary, by which Chou meant that the Ladakh salient, which lies north of the Himalayan chain, could be placed in the balance against the Indian North-East Frontier Agency, which lies south of it. The Six Points had been intended to forestall the examination of evidence demanded by India; and when they failed to do so the Chinese officials could only urge that different principles should apply to different local situations. The later attempt by the *Kwangming Daily* to dispense altogether with natural principles in border-delimitation suggested in some quarters that clarification had been required by party or public opinion inside China, since the watershed principle had been accepted in the settlements with Burma, Nepal and Pakistan. But the expert services of Chang Hung-tseng may equally have been needed to meet in advance any Soviet argument that the natural frontier of the Amur and Ussuri Rivers was to be respected for its own sake.

In dismissing ideas of a natural frontier Chang Hung-tseng made much of the fact that people of Tibetan stock had in the past made their way over the watershed and 'spread to many places on the southern side of the Himalayas'. Following this, he asserted, 'the administrative jurisdiction of the Tibet region of China has extended to these places'. The threat implied in this proposition might be felt not only in parts of the NEFA, in Bhutan, Sikkim and Nepal, but also beyond the frontiers of Sinkiang where the Chinese had before 1860 had moveable pickets for the control of Kazakh pasture-lands extending far from the mountain-alignment which subsequently became the border. On the other hand Chou En-lai had welcomed, in the settlement with Burma, the fact that elements of the same national grouping existed on both sides of the border. This, he said, would make for friendly relations.

In the case of Burma it may be judged that Chinese manipulation of such a situation would not be impeded by a boundary-agreement. In the case of India and the Himalayan States, stalemate itself offers opportunities for Chinese pressure, with Bhutan as the most vulnerable area. In the Central Asian frontier-zone, however, the Chinese remain at a distinct disadvantage. The inducement for Soviet subversion is a powerful one, and the removal from power of Khrushchev, to whom the Chinese had personally attributed responsibility for the 'frontier-provocations', produced no signs of a basic resolution of the conflict.

X

FRONTIERS IN A NEW ERA

A NUCLEAR POSTURE

AFTER fifteen years of Communist rule, China entered 1965 with a nuclear certificate of great-power status. To countries lying under the real or fancied threat of Chinese expansion what mattered was not the timing of the first and long-expected test-explosion (16 October 1964), nor even its evaluation by military technologists, but its political purpose. Peking's official explanations expressed this purpose in two ways, both of which were ostensibly equated with the preservation of world peace. The development of Chinese nuclear capability would provide 'great encouragement to the revolutionary peoples of the world in their struggles'; and it would 'break the nuclear monopoly of the nuclear powers'. In other words the Soviet nuclear strength, which Peking had been accustomed to extol as a *bloc* asset in the service of revolutionary struggle, was no longer regarded as having broken a Western monopoly. It was by implication a partner in a monopoly which it had been left for China to break. The effort to break it had been necessary because the Soviet Government had declined to put its own weight behind enterprises which in the Chinese view were both ideologically sound and essential to the defence of Chinese territory.

The identification of a programme of world revolution with Chinese geopolitical aspirations was in no sense new. It could be traced as a dynamic impulse in Mao's long career, from the day that the Karakhan Declaration helped to turn him into a Communist. Now that that career was approaching its natural term there was evidence of an internal effort to preserve the doctrine after his death, while the external campaign against his Moscow rivals showed no disposition towards compromise. The declaration that a Chinese nuclear capability had only defensive, or retaliatory, aims, had to be interpreted against this background. An ideologically aggressive policy at the service of a territorially unsatisfied Power contained all the seeds of future frontier-conflict.

The possession of nuclear weapons, however, had no clear or direct bearing upon the winning of frontier-wars —a conclusion which the Chinese were prepared to cite from the late President Kennedy himself. What the demonstrative test in the Lop Nor region had done was to signpost China's route of advance towards international recognition on her own and no one else's terms. As in the past, so in the future, her political struggle to attain a self-chosen destiny was of dire concern to the tenants of convenient battlefields beyond her borders. The real problems of Vietnam, for instance, had small chance of being solved, or even closely considered, in the heat of China's rivalries with the United States and the Soviet Union; and a plan like the Mekong Valley Project, of immense possibilities for the whole area, could be made to appear not merely irrelevant but even hostile to the doctrine that 'politics must take command'. From the general field of Chinese propaganda the theme of frontier-claims had in the meantime temporarily disappeared.

MAPS UNDER REVISION

The new editions of Chinese maps published during 1964 had the familiar effect of obscuring more questions than they answered. But on the assumption of at least a partial intention to instruct, certain features have to be noticed. The 1964 *Map of the Chinese People's Republic* appears as the third revised edition of the 1956 map, which in the dispute with India had been stated by Chou En-lai (letter to Nehru, 17 December 1959) to show correctly what the Chinese regarded as the boundary between the two countries.

The first revision of this map in 1960, when produced by the Chinese official team in the course of the joint investigations, had greatly contributed to the Indian mistrust of the Chinese case and intentions: first because it extended the already disputed 1956 claim of China in Ladakh by several thousand square miles; and secondly because, although the Indian team had been able to indicate this difference of alignment with precision, the Chinese Government declined, both then and later, to explain or even acknowledge the divergence. As was to be expected, this advanced 1960 claim-line is incorporated once more in the Chinese boundaries as presented in the 1964 map. The alignment west of the Karakoram Pass, which the Chinese were not willing to include in their 1960 discussions with India, was eventually negotiated with Pakistan and finds its place in the 1964 revision of the map of China. In those negotiations, as we have seen, the Chinese were prepared for some retreat from the extreme positions in the Karakoram region which they had claimed cartographically in 1960.

By the terms on which both China and Pakistan undertook negotiations on this portion of the Chinese boundaries, the result was to be regarded as provisional, pending a solution of the Kashmir dispute between Pakistan and India. Nevertheless publicity was given in January 1965 to the process of an apparently permanent demarcation on the ground. Following a precedent which had recently been set on the Sino-Nepalese frontier, inscribed concrete posts were fixed at points of formidably difficult access in the presence of representatives of both sides. And in the 1964 *Map of the People's Republic of China* no allowance is made for the provisional nature of the agreement with Pakistan. The frontier carries the marking for 'determined'.

Even more curiously, the 'determined' marking is carried along the entire extent of China's southern frontiers as seen by Peking. Thus, on the one hand, Bhutan is allowed as firm a national boundary as Sikkim and Nepal; and on the other the basis of China's dispute with India (that the frontier was 'nowhere determined') is to all appearances relinquished. Instead, the boundaries with India have been unilaterally 'determined' by taking in the full extent of China's claims, not only in the strategically coveted and largely occupied Ladakh salient, but also in the 32,000 square miles of 'bargaining area' south of the McMahon Line which remains fully in India's control.

What was 'undetermined' by the Peking cartographers in 1964 is also notable. It includes for instance, the whole of China's frontier with the Mongolian People's Republic, the settlement of which had been firmly announced at the end of 1962. In the zone of Central Asian contact with the USSR the 'undetermined' marking is partially employed, from the Pamir northwards to the Karatash Pass. On this evidence Chinese irredentism would seem to be more concerned with Sinkiang's borders with the Soviet Tadzhik and Kirghiz Republics than with recovery of 'the Great North-West' from Kazakhstan. The interpretation of the north-eastern Sino-Soviet frontier, and of the Sino-Korean frontier, is unclear.

The outlook suggested by the new *Concise Geography of China*, published in Peking towards the end of 1964, is similar but not identical. The same 'determination' of China's southern frontiers is asserted, but the frontier with the Mongolian People's Republic is this time indicated as fixed. The undefined section of the Central Asian frontier is repeated. More significantly, perhaps, the single folding map, taken together with those in the text, leave undefined the entire north-eastern boundaries of China: the boundaries with the Soviet Union along the Amur (Heilung-kiang) and the Ussuri Rivers, and with Korea along the Yalu.

This would seem to keep in being the Chinese claim to the Manchu Empire's 'Great North-East', marked in Liu Pei-hua's map of Chinese irridenta as having been ceded to Russia in the 'unequal' treaties of Aigun (1858) and Peking (1860). But whereas Liu Pei-hua's book and map had eventually, after adverse international publicity, to be disavowed, the 1964 *Concise Geography* (by Jen Yu-ti) was published in English and other languages, specifically for external information, by the official Foreign Languages Press in Peking. Without raising any more questions of what happened to the Manchu Empire it preserved, in this north-eastern area at least, a deliberate ambiguity. It also described both Hong Kong and Kow-loon as 'part of Chinese territory', adding the information that 'the U.S. imperialists and Chiang Kai-shek agents use Hong Kong to carry out their criminal hostile activities against the Chinese people'. Finally, its map designates a maritime boundary for China which, after taking in Taiwan, continues southwards through the China Sea for some 1,500 miles, and then bends north again to skirt Vietnam. At its farthest reach this scoops up more blue water and small islands than Liu Pei-hua had assigned to the Manchu Empire at its climax. It might be regarded as the retort of a non-naval Power to the U.S. Seventh Fleet. But at the same time, in reasserting a Chinese possession of the Paracel Islands, it conflicts with a Vietnamese claim to which patriots in Hanoi and Saigon are equally attached.

NEW LOOK AT THE NORTH-EAST

Whether deliberately or not, these maps drew more attention to the alienation of China's 'Great North-East' than of her 'Great North-West'. The same could certainly be said of the world-map, to emphasize the positions and extent of China and Mexico, which at the turn of 1963–4 was distributed with a publicity-booklet at the Chinese Trade Fair in Mexico City. Though broadly drawn, this map unquestionably included the Soviet Maritime Territories within China's frontiers, but without advancing any claim on Outer Mongolia or in Central Asia.

The trend of China's north-eastern outlook was apparent in the interviews to which a delegation of Japanese Socialists was treated by both Mao Tse-tung and Chou En-lai in the summer of 1964. In allowing himself to be quoted as an advocate for the return of the Kurile Islands to Japan, Mao was reversing his Government's previous approval of the transfer to the Soviet Union, in accordance with the Yalta provisions, of the Kuriles and the southern half of the long island of Sakhalin. The latter, though too far north to appear on most general Chinese maps, had figured in more than one list of 'lost' Chinese imperial territories—and similarly, as *Pravda* indignantly noted, in Liu

Pei-hua's notorious compilation. But in fact what Sakhalin can show of history is a matter of Russian and Japanese penetration, from north and south respectively, of a grim and sparsely-peopled land. An uneasy condominium had been replaced by Russian acquisition in 1875, when the Treaty of St Petersburg acknowledged in return that the Kuriles were Japanese. Defeated by the Japanese in 1904, the Russians ceded to them the southern half of Sakhalin. The Tsar's discomfiture had been a matter of satisfaction to the Russian revolutionaries: which did not prevent Stalin, at the Yalta Conference in February 1945, from demanding and obtaining from his Western Allies an agreement to restore 'the former rights of Russia violated by the treacherous attack of Japan in 1904'. These were specified to include the southern part of Sakhalin. The transfer to Russia of the Kuriles, which was pure booty, was provided for in a separate clause.

The remaining items in this almost effortless recovery of the Russian Empire in the Far East had been provided at Chinese expense. But if the pains of 'leaning to one side' were apparent in Mao's subsequent confirmation of the arrangement, his Soviet alliance had offered him the compensating expectations, not only of improving China's position by negotiation, but of guaranteeing it against a Japanese resurgence. No other assailant of modern times had come so near as Japan to the actual conquest of China. And Communist theory was at hand to make such a revival plausible, for it cast Japanese militarism in a new rôle as an instrument of American imperialism. In August 1951, when the Yalta clauses affecting Japan were officially endorsed by Peking, the Chinese People's Government had good reason to prefer that the strategic Kuriles should be under Soviet, rather than Japanese or American control. For the Communist adventure in Korea had brought American forces and their United Nations associates, with rear headquarters in Japan, to the Chinese frontier itself.

By 1964 the picture was seen to have changed. A new tone towards Japan was emerging from the Chinese conviction that Khrushchev's Soviet Union was an unreliable and even a treacherous ally against the designated American enemy. The detachment of Japan from the United States had hitherto been sought by subversive propaganda and the support of extremist groups and movements in the Japanese opposition. These tactics were not discarded, and indeed Peking was by now gaining from Moscow within the perennially split Japanese Communist Party. But there were simultaneous explorations, at commercial and semi-official levels, towards normal State-relationships. The former Japanese imperial fief of Korea was not for disposal. Beyond their semi-frontier on the Yalu the Chinese had at last loosened the tenacious Soviet grip on Kim Il Sung's Party and Government; and beyond Kim Il Sung's semi-frontier at the 38th parallel they continued to treat Japanese political approaches to South Korea as a return (under U.S. pressure) to the old path of militarist aggression. But the question of the Kuriles, in the context of Soviet land-grabbing, had now become 'clear' to Mao and his colleagues. 'They must be returned to Japan.'

If this meant anything it meant that the imperialist menace to China's territorial integrity—the 'intervention' expected by the logic of Communism—was deemed to have receded. With it had gone the protective value of Soviet bases in the Kuriles, and of the military commitments of the Sino-Soviet alliance for which in 1950 Mao had been prepared to shelve so many basic Chinese claims against Russia. The specific Soviet undertaking had been to join with the Chinese People's Government in resisting any attack by Japan or a Power allied with Japan. At certain times of stress—notably in 1958—Khrushchev had found it appropriate to reaffirm that 'an attack on the Chinese People's Republic would be an attack on the Soviet Union'. But in the summer of 1962, when 'frenzied war-preparations' by the United States and its Japanese collaborator proved (according to Peking) the *intention* to attack the Chinese mainland from Taiwan or elsewhere, Khrushchev contented himself, if not his allies, with a vague assurance of 'combat fraternity and comradely solidarity'. More significantly he had resisted every Chinese attempt to invest the Soviet commitment with something more than a defensive function. American protection of the Nationalist stronghold of Taiwan was something to be denounced, but not something to be remedied by force with the approval, still less the assistance, of the Soviet Union. The existence of a border-dispute with India was not to bear the interpretation of a violation of Chinese territory and a *casus belli* for the Sino-Soviet alliance. Nor were the Chinese entitled, under the larger cover of Marx-Leninist doctrine, to discover a revolutionary situation wherever it suited them, and to demand its exploitation without reference to the international—and thermonuclear —consequences.

INDO-CHINA AS A FRONTIER-ZONE

The region in which Chinese, Soviet and American interests were to become so intricately and dangerously grappled was that of the historic overspill of Chinese population and influence into South-East Asia. Yet here, where they seemed the most porous, the actual frontiers of China were the least contentious. The area beyond them, unlike that of Korea, has carried no past or present threat to Chinese territory: although in Chinese memories the former French trade, railway and mining-concessions in Yunnan and Kwangsi may stand in much the same light. It is the northward look of China's neighbour-peoples that has been justifiably wary. Resistance to Chinese penetration, political, cultural or physical, has not lost its force in the nationalism which in North Vietnam accepted and succumbed to Communist direction. The early temptations of Titoism were resisted, but only because the link with Moscow seemed to offer the better safeguard, as well as a level of material aid unobtainable from other Communist sources.

So long as Sino-Soviet differences could be kept out of Hanoi's internal polemics, the necessary balance worked well enough. And for various reasons Ho Chi Minh proved more difficult to dislodge from a fence-sitting posture than Kim Il Sung. In both Korea and Vietnam the Chinese were theoretically well placed, as the advocates and tacticians of a virile revolutionary policy, to appropriate the southward momentum of 'national reunification'. In both cases they encouraged ideological notions of 'self-reliance' in order to weaken party dependence on Moscow. In the North Korean system, though the pro-Soviet elements had survived several party purges, Kim Il Sung exercised a sufficiently close control to swerve towards the Chinese — and back again — when necessary. In North Vietnam the evidence of Communist fission remained even when Ho Chi Minh's middle course was seen to have been politically undermined. But the evidence of action followed quickly, in a new and serious testing of the will of the United States to retain its commitments to South Vietnam.

However that critical heightening of tension might have been initiated, there was no doubt that it promoted Peking's own challenge to Moscow, in a field which offered the greatest prospects of Soviet embarrassment, and for China an acceptable balance of risks and opportunities. The most obvious risk was that of provoking operations in which China's own territory might be subjected to crippling attack. Against this China's assurance was not, of course, her own state of progress towards nuclear capability but those 'lessons of Korea' which in the first months of 1965 were much recommended to American attention by Chinese propaganda. The Korean experience, for example, had shown that the exercise of American military, and especially nuclear, preponderance was subject in practice to political limitations. It had exhibited, moreover, a Chinese determination to preserve a belt of territory beyond her frontier from invasion by hostile forces. Peking's hints or declarations of intent in the Vietnam crisis could consequently be broken down thus:

(i) In the event of attack upon her own territory, China would not shrink from war on any scale demanded.

(ii) If the forward zone of Chinese defence represented by the North Vietnam People's Republic should be 'invaded' (i.e. by ground-forces) China 'would not stand idly by'—a repetition of an attitude previously announced in respect of the adjacent frontier-kingdom of Laos.

Short of this, the more violent the conflict and the greater the American involvement, the surer seemed the promise of political gains for China. Seen from Peking, the eventual elimination of United States power from this part of Asia might be a matter of dogmatic confidence. But it would have value only if it were achieved without substantial Soviet intervention, since the elimination of Soviet power was also required. In this context the important difference between the Vietnamese and the Korean frontier-areas was openly acknowledged in July 1965 when *Pravda* pointed out the absence of any direct Soviet land-communication with Vietnam. The difference was of no less moment for Ho Chi Minh, for whom re-unification would be a hollow success if the struggle should bring Chinese land-forces across the fraternal frontier.

THE PRIVILEGE OF PACIFICATION

To the south of that undisturbed frontier of her own, China's claim to a sphere of influence had been much concerned with the fluctuating borders between lesser peoples. In the pattern of pacification envisaged by the Geneva settlement, the Chinese could see little prospect of improving their position except by first encouraging the disturbance of such tranquillity as there was, and then pressing for the 'neutralization' of Laos and other political units under international guarantee. A shared responsibility for the destinies of the South-East Asian peninsula, however, could hardly be regarded by China as the ideal solution, or as more than a temporary one.

The traditional Chinese concept of a paramount rôle in this region represented the Dragon Throne as the sole and natural arbiter in the contentious affairs of the *Nan-yang*, the inferior peoples of the South. 'They love to fight among themselves,' says a Chinese text of honoured antiquity (the Sui-shu). 'Therefore they are weak countries, and from time to time acknowledge the supremacy of China.'*

This quarrelsome propensity, such as it was, was subdued or obscured in the 19th-century advance of British and French dominion. But the pacifying function in the Chinese tradition has not been forgotten, and the technique of producing situations inviting its exercise has been greatly developed. By the testimony of Liu Pei-hua's map, Western pacification was as much an infraction of China's rights when it took the form of an Anglo-French guarantee of the independence of Siam (Thailand), as in the colonial administration of Burma, Indochina and the Malay States. The phase of Japanese occupation in the Second World War (in which Thailand continued to enjoy a preferential position) fell into the same category. Indeed it was part of the pattern of aggression against China, and detachment of her provinces, which had begun in Manchuria.

An altogether new picture followed the defeat of Japan's bid for regional supremacy, since China had the status of a partner—if treated as a junior one—in the elimination of Japan. And Chiang Kai-shek, so soon as an Allied victory appeared to be in sight, had staked the claim of a re-emergent China to a share in guaranteeing the post-war independence of both Burma and Indochina. His Communist supplanters pursued a different path, but without losing sight of the goal. And in the relationship eventually developed with Burma they could no doubt feel that they

---

* O. W. Wolters, from whom this quotation is borrowed, makes the interesting observation that 'for reasons which are still not quite clear, the accession of a new and powerful Chinese dynasty always seemed to coincide with a period of temporary political upheaval in South-East Asia' (*China Irredenta: the South*, in *The World Today*, December 1963. Royal Institute of International Affairs).

had improved on Chiang's modest proposal for a place in a Concert of Powers.

To the east of Burma, however, China's acknowledged share in the security of the fragmented landscape over-looked from her borders was still a small one, and difficult to implement. She had participated in the international settlement, made far away in Geneva, which gave a formal satisfaction to national aspirations in the area relinquished by France. But the supporting apparatus, framed to reduce the risks of a clash between two power-blocs, left the United Kingdom and Soviet Russia in the position of joint-Chairmen, with India, Poland and Canada supplying the local supervision. And at the same time the fear of revived Chinese ambitions brought a new guarantor into the picture, when Thailand found collective protection for her independence—and her not undisputed frontiers—in a combination headed by the United States. South Viet-nam, Cambodia, even China's border-kingdom of Laos, were tempted by protocol—and by a common apprehen-sion—into the same system. And the tale of new and old States asserting their interest in the security of the South-East Asian peninsula swelled intolerably. The full force of Chinese political warfare was directed upon this appar-ently confused and vulnerable collection of safeguards against both aggression and subversion. But its consider-able effectiveness in its primary purposes, over nearly a decade, received some tribute in the development of Chinese diplomatic techniques. And the cautious progress of Peking's efforts to detach Cambodia from the alien pattern was cited, in Chinese political directives, in the same terms as the relations achieved with Burma.

Of all the signs that Cambodia's insurance-cover was being gradually transferred from Washington to Peking,

none was more symbolic than Prince Sihanouk's convey-
ance to the Chinese capital, towards the end of 1964, of a
frontier-grievance against the Republic of South Vietnam
on which he had appealed without success to the International Control Commission and to the United Nations.
The delegations to which China was host represented the
Cambodian Government, the North Vietnam Government
in Hanoi, and in South Vietnam the Vietcong 'National
Liberation Front'. What Cambodia was seeking, on the
eve of the intensified Vietcong military enterprise,
amounted to Chinese protection against the revival under
Communist auspices of the old southward dynamism of
the Vietnamese. The results were not decisive, but the
gesture accorded with that image of a natural Chinese
paramountcy which Peking had cherished for so long. It
was quickly followed by the despatch to Cambodia of
Chinese arms.

Within this general picture of outlying peoples jostling
each other in the Chinese shadow, the tiny frontier upon
which an ideological 'containment' of Communist expansion had come to rest seemed topographically irrelevant, a
theoretical confrontation along a fifty-mile cease-fire line
at the 17th parallel, the waist of an hour-glass. Sooner or
later, it might have been argued, something more realistic
would come to be substituted, such as the Mekong River.
If so, the Chinese were ready with hints that Thailand
would be next on the list for a crisis. The curiously open
nature of these suggestions seemed designed less to foment
internal rebellion than to persuade the Thai Government
to trim its sails in the manner of Sihanouk's Cambodia.

THE KASHMIR SYNDROME

At the other extreme of China's long southern frontiers, in the vast mountain-belt of Kashmir, the contentious character of outlying peoples had also been displayed. There was even, at the end of March 1965, an opportunity to hint that for these bickerings, as for those to be expected of the *Nan-yang*, Peking could provide an appropriate tribunal. This was in the curious episode of the Chinese approaches to Sheikh Abdullah, the veteran spokesman of a relatively independent and nationalist Kashmiri aspiration. In this case, however, the gesture could be more plausibly explained as a contribution to a useful state of dispute than as the assertion of a Chinese right to resolve it. In an area where China's frontier-interests are mainly and vitally strategic, the profits that she can expect from rivalries beyond her border have been made to seem obvious. Yet even when China's increasingly close relations with Pakistan had become a normal factor in international calculation, it was still difficult for her critics, especially in India, to appreciate the almost inevitable rôle which the Kashmir dispute had played in Chinese frontier-policies.

The difficulty was expressed at its simplest in a sense of outrage, first at the treachery of China's hostility towards a friendly and non-aligned India; and secondly at her apparent flouting of her own ideological principles in amicable dealings with Pakistan, a State which from an early date had proscribed its Communist Party, joined anti-Communist combinations such as SEATO and CENTO, and accepted military aid from the United States. Yet it is obvious that Marxist teaching had from the beginning combined with national self-interest to form a Chinese attitude towards the new States of the Indian sub-continent. In 1949, indeed, there had been little except Marxist theory to illuminate this alien scene for men who had for years been preoccupied in the peculiar isolation of their own struggle for power.

The emergence of independent India and Pakistan, a development of cardinal importance when viewed from outside China, was thus heavily devalued in Peking. In itself it could represent no qualitative change. Nor was there a *prima facie* case for preferring either of the two new régimes to the other. Both must be categorized in identical terms of class-structure and political tendency, as the bourgeois beneficiaries of uncompleted revolution. Yet for the Chinese Communists there was one significant point of difference between India and Pakistan, a basic difference of dimension. As the larger and more powerful State, India was the major heir of an imperialism not yet liqui-dated, inheriting long frontiers with the greater China and certain unacceptable interests in Tibet. This was what Chou En-lai was later to call 'a dark side' to Sino-Indian relations, existing 'from the beginning'. It was confirmed by the Nehru Government's early steps to renew the formerly subsisting treaty-links with Bhutan and Sikkim, to declare its interest in the preservation of Nepal, and to exercise the privilege of critical comment on the Chinese move into Tibet. And an orthodox presumption of the new India's political colour had already been spelled out in the congratulations which Mao had blandly accepted from the Communist Party of India, slightly in advance of the credentials of India's first Ambassador.*

* 'The toiling masses of India feel jubilant over this great victory. They know it hastens their own liberation. They are inspired by it to fight more determinedly and courageously their battle for ending the present régime and establishing the rule of People's Democracy. . . . I wish to assure you, and

In this initial view from Peking, therefore, although Pakistan was ideologically a chip off the old imperialist block she was, after all, a chip. The block was India. The very existence of Pakistan demonstrated that the material was fissionable. The dispute over Kashmir had carried the crack into the frontier-zone in the region of prime import-ance to the Chinese. In the northern marches of a State artificially created by China's imperial rivals—first the Sikhs and then the British—there was restored something of that normal and desirable condition of division which had maintained the concept of Chinese power with annual tributes of gold-dust and silken scarves. Half a century before the establishment of the Chinese People's Republic, a moribund Manchu Empire had declined the opportunity of a frontier-settlement* which would have bequeathed to Mao Tse-tung in 1949 security for Sinkiang along the Karakoram watershed and enough of the uninhabited Ladakh salient to provide the strategic communication with Tibet. To have accepted it would have trenched upon a Chinese feudal interest, as Peking saw it, in the petty kingdom of Hunza. It would also have recognized a unit-ary empire as China's direct neighbour along the whole frontier from the Pamir to Nepal. If the Chinese Com-munists, in their eventual border-agreement with Pakistan, appeared for once to regard archaic tributary relation-ships as negotiable, it was doubtless because the fact and function of fragmentation was preserved by the very act of dealing separately with Pakistan.

---

through you the people of China, that the Communist Party of India will unmask all the anti-Chinese intrigues that the Nehru Government might hatch under the dictates of the American imperialists and rally the people to defeat them.'—*Message from B. T. Ranadive, General Secretary of the CPI, to Mao Tse-tung, 12 October 1949.*

* On the so-called Macartney-MacDonald alignment of 1899 (see above, p. 100).

The Chinese investigations of the prospect of a special relationship with Pakistan began at least as early as 1955; when Chou En-lai, having secured an Indian agreement on Tibet without yielding any firm or specific assurance about the frontier, took the opportunity of the Bandung Conference for private talks with the Pakistan Prime Minister. Considered from the Chinese side alone, a successful exploitation of the dispute in Kashmir would depend upon the degree to which Western imperialism would itself be able to profit from this situation, as in any Communist analysis it must fully intend to do. But however one may analyse the subsequent development of Chinese policy and its reaction to events (and to non-events), what was withheld from Pakistan is as significant as what was conceded. What was withheld (until August 1965) was the support of her case in the Kashmir question. Khrushchev's declaration of a Soviet recognition of the Indian claim had in this sense played into the Chinese hand: since a non-committal silence was enough to place China in a relatively favourable position with Pakistan, and to leave untouched the fact of division on which Chinese frontier-policy would continue to rely.

STALEMATE IN THE SOUTH

Such are the bases of the new Chinese pragmatism, in success and in failure. Since it must be clear that with a different policy and outlook the Chinese Communists could have secured without conflict, by early and frank discussion with an Indian Government disposed to accommodation, a satisfactory alignment in this key-sector of the frontier, the story might be accounted a tragic failure. In their own terms, however, the Chinese could by 1965 congratulate themselves on the overcoming of formidable difficulties and critical opposition in the fulfilment of their 1950 directive to the armed forces: to liberate Tibet and stand on the frontiers of the Republic.

More positively, the Peking communiqué of 25 October 1950 had expressed the intention to 'consolidate national defence on the western borders of China'—in other words to organize the protection of Sinkiang against the new Russian ally with whom China was at that moment collaborating in the Korean adventure. On the southern flank of this immensely extended strategy the Chinese had chosen to regard their frontiers as so fluid that their first occupation-forces moved in many cases without maps, or at least without frontier-references. In place of this they now had a southern frontier established and garrisoned to their apparent satisfaction, always assuming that their unfulfilled demands south of the McMahon Line had been and remained a limited political instrument.

Following a broadly intelligible watershed course, which nevertheless left the advantages of terrain in Chinese hands, this southern frontier was now supported either by the agreements with Pakistan, Nepal and Burma, or by the effect of military stalemate with India along a 'line of actual control'. And this line of control, not seriously impaired by the twenty-kilometre withdrawal principle, represented in the important Ladakh sector the actual conquest of a zone of security a good deal broader than earlier Chinese strategy had thought necessary. In February 1964 the Indian Government charged the Chinese in this sector with abusing the sanction of 'civilian checkposts' in the Colombo proposals by setting up marking-cairns along the limits of their 1962 advance. The allegation was refuted by Peking, but not in an entirely conclusive manner. And in any case the Chinese intention of arguing from the basis of this military gain in any return to negotiation had been apparent in their acceptance of the Colombo proposals 'in principle' as against the Indian acceptance *'in toto'*. There was thus no sign of the minimum expectation of an area of compromise which would enable any Indian Government to renew discussions. And suggestions from academic sources that the old and much argued 'Macartney-MacDonald alignment' furnished a concession that India ought not now to refuse, became less and less relevant as the Chinese built themselves in on a considerably deeper line.

In the meantime the strengthening of the Indian defence-potential—an elaborate, almost ruinously expensive but unavoidable commitment—continued the process of militarizing the whole frontier which the Chinese had initiated. The warily-accepted insulation-strip between the advanced forces of both sides was in general more effective than the continuing allegations of intrusion might suggest. But the nature of the country on which such limits were theoretically drawn has to be borne in mind; and at several points in both western and eastern sectors their alignment was in any case in dispute. On the Sikkim frontier, where the question of a 'zone of withdrawal' did not arise, fortification of the passes produced frequent complaints of trespass. If the Indians continued, after their experience of 1962, to expect and prepare for another invasion in strength, the Chinese could now consider themselves reasonably secured even against the infiltration by forward Indian defence-posts and patrols which in 1961 and 1962 had disturbed their own advances in Ladakh. For the Chinese position, apart from its topographical advantage, enjoyed political safeguards.

One safeguard was provided by the differences between

India and Pakistan which Peking was so naturally and obviously concerned to preserve and extend; and most conspicuously by the unresolved dispute in Kashmir, where India's strategic communications as yet possessed no fully satisfactory alternative to the route through Srinagar in the contentious Vale. The other safeguard was furnished, somewhat ironically, by the Western military commitments to India which Chinese aggression had provoked. For this support would be available neither for the Indian 'expansionism' on which Chinese propaganda continued to dilate, nor even (so far as could be known) for the recovery of any of the territory on which the Chinese now stood. If a dogmatically non-aligned India had modified her outlook sufficiently to accept this unexpressed condition, a dogmatically Communist China had gained sufficient international experience to appreciate it.

Any connection between China's decision to develop a nuclear weapon and her policy on this frontier would have to be dated from the taking of the decision, at least as early as 1959, and not from October 1964, when the first test was made. From the urgency which the test-explosion must lend to the general international question of nuclear proliferation Peking would expect its own political profit. The particular debate that must arise in India could be calculated, however it might turn, to strengthen right-wing demands for a more positive stand against China. Yet there could hardly be more anti-Chinese policies than those which Peking continued to attribute to Nehru's successors through all available channels. And on the 'line of actual control' even a theoretically aggressive India would be held in check by the governing facts of the situation.

Behind this relatively stabilized frontier the argument,

as it had always been, was about power; and the initiative remained in important respects, as it had always done, with the Chinese. But the line which India could directly guard with the help of friendly Powers was not continuous. Where it involved the integrity of the frontier-States political factors came into play, with Bhutan (whose pro-Indian Prime Minister had been assassinated in April 1964) as the softest area below the watershed. Here and elsewhere within the grope of their 'Five Fingers' theory the Chinese were undeniably well placed for subversion, and well practiced in it also. The contrivance of a situation which might extend their control towards the foothills without directly testing Indian resistance was a continual possibility. Indeed the idea that control by the Chinese was only a matter of time was one which had for years been deliberately sown among the frontier-peoples.

THE PROBLEM OF DISAFFECTION

It seems probable that a programme of this kind, and its timing, would be more closely influenced by developments in Tibet than by developments in India. The Chinese Communists have their own worries about subversion, clearly detectable beneath wild accusations of Indian responsibility for the Tibetan rebellion. In abandoning, early in 1965, the formality of keeping a place in Lhasa open for the eventual return of the Dalai Lama from 'abduction', the Chinese were relinquishing the last hope of turning the prestige of the revered exile to the advantage of their own internal administration. Shortly afterwards the Panchen Lama was himself relieved of the shadow of authority inside Tibet, and placed under house-arrest by the Chinese, whose methods of ruthless suppression had presumably been carried beyond the limits of connivance which that unfortunate young man could allow himself.* Tibetan reactions to these moves were strong enough to produce fresh reports of serious disturbance after many months of virtual silence; and even, at the end of July, an official admission from the Chinese radio at Lhasa, in the usual form of an announcement that rebellion had been crushed. The picture that could be pieced together indicated armed resistance conducted not only from isolated mountain-redoubts to the west, north and north-east of Lhasa, but in something like a chain of operations over a frontier-belt covering the eastern half of the Nepal border and the sectors adjoining Sikkim and Bhutan, and thence widening in a threat to Chinese communications and convoys in the area between Lhasa and the McMahon Line.

Making every allowance for the exaggerations of rumour, it could be concluded that the temper of the ill-used Tibetans and the rugged nature of their vast country were blemishes on its conversion from a war-occupied territory to a workable 'autonomous region' of China. The Chinese airfields and garrisons have multiplied; the great lateral roads link metropolitan China with its precious western development-areas; their network of southward spurs has already transformed the military and political geography of the Himalayan region. Yet here, rather than on that Aksai Chin plateau for which the Chinese have been ready to fight their largest Asian neighbour, the arteries of power remain vulnerable. In Tibet it is the enemy that has displayed the theoretically invincible combination of national fervour with guerilla tactics, the Chinese motorized and airborne forces which have been revealed as paper tigers.

---

* The last straw had reportedly been a Chinese demand that he should publicly denounce the Dalai Lama, a compliance not to be secured even by a lifetime of Chinese tutelage.

Until this situation is definitively changed in her favour, China's policy and tactics in contiguous and ethnically related Himalayan regions seems likely to be guided more by the aim of sealing off the resisters than of adding to their numbers. Such an aim could in itself involve disturbance of the present frontier-position, but not under the conditions which a purely acquisitive intention would dictate.

In the larger sense, also, the Chinese view of frontier-questions continued to be publicly linked with the problems of controlling the non-Chinese peoples whose homelands account for almost all the border-marches. A repetition of insurrection in Sinkiang, of the kind which gave point to the first Chinese denunciations of Russian frontiers and frontier-policies in 1963, could bring the topic back into a Sino-Soviet controversy which has shown no signs of wilting for lack of it. It is even possible that the apparent abandonment of China's claims upon Outer Mongolia, by the boundary-agreement with the Mongolian People's Republic, had as one of its aims a greater facility for China's control of the Mongolians on her own side of the line. However that may be, there has been no really strong reason to dismiss the occasional protestations of the Chinese Communists that they were more concerned to exploit and populate their 'empty lands' than to seek outlets beyond them for the pressure of numbers. Official Chinese attitudes to demographic problems, and to birth-control, have fluctuated considerably. But the only occasion on which a connection with frontier-questions has been allowed to appear was the curious and unexplained incident of 1963, when for some weeks the Chinese authorities permitted—if they did not actively induce—thousands of their undernourished subjects to clamour for refuge in the already densely populated British colony of Hong Kong.

PRAGMATISM AND PATIENCE

To the outside world Hong Kong bears the aspect of the crowning symbol of Chinese pragmatism—or Chinese patience. Its very existence seems to perpetuate, in the leased hardly less than in the ceded territory, the situation of national helplessness which the Chinese are bent on expunging from their history. Its prosperity and tranquillity might well appear to the rulers of China as an exposure of their system and an affront to their reputation. Seen in that light, extinction of the affront would inflict a commensurate loss of face upon the Western world. From the purely military viewpoint, moreover, this is a point at which Chinese 'frontier-rectification', as it would no doubt be called, could be accomplished in a few days, if not in a few hours. But the practical arguments against such an enterprise are no less obvious. Nearly half of the People's Republic's entire and sorely-needed supply of foreign exchange comes from Hong Kong, either directly in the payment for exports or indirectly in remittances from Chinese overseas through the Hong Kong banks. And this is only the most immediately calculable function of an economic and political air-vent without which the Chinese Communist State could hardly have survived either the catastrophes of the Great Leap Forward or the breach with the Soviet Union. Even the foreign espionage, of which Hong Kong appears as a swarming nest in Chinese accounts, is balanced by the reciprocal opportunities available to Peking.

In a sense, also, the military vulnerability of Hong Kong enables the Chinese Communists to tolerate its existence with a minimum of damage to their revolutionary image as the redressors of past 'inequality'—the assumed capacity for 'rectification' serving here the same purpose as the act itself. It was the ability to take action at a time of China's own choosing which furnished the retort to Soviet taunts on the subject. On another front where the acquisition of territory was not a fundamental Chinese need, in the Eastern Himalayan region, India had been left to reflect upon this ability; and the intention to press even larger claims against the Soviet Union itself had equally been expressed as if the timing rested upon Peking's sole decision. Like all such 'open' questions, that of Hong Kong might at some appropriate moment strengthen China's negotiating position on the climb to international power.

The similar, but more curious, license allowed to Portugal in the matter of Macao led to a number of reports during 1965 that the enclave was serving as a counter in preliminary negotiations for recognition between Peking and Lisbon. What was unconcealed, at all events, was the equivocal ideological position which the Chinese delegation to the Helsinki meeting of the World Peace Congress (July 1965) found itself called upon to defend. Against Communists speaking in the name of Portugal and the Portuguese colonies in Africa, and loudly demanding that Macao should be returned to China as an act of 'liberation from imperialism', the Chinese had much ado to delete the subject from the agenda as that of 'a different kind of colony', an internal affair to be resolved as and when Peking should determine.

'When the time is ripe.' The phrase has been made ominous by frontier-conflicts already precipitated and by the extended time-scale which habitually characterizes

Chinese pronouncements. The long view has important uses. It is employed to stimulate national and party confidence without arousing dangerous expectations in any one generation. On territorial questions, as on those of internal progress, it can help to tide over setbacks and reduce the side-effects of cumulative propaganda. The prolonged ineffectiveness of Peking's emphatic claims upon Taiwan, for example, might have been expected to depress morale in the People's Army, on whom the liberation of the island had been impressed as a principal duty. The explanatory programme of the Army's Central Political Department accordingly included in one of its confidential Work Bulletins (dated April 1961), a remarkably succinct statement of attitude: 'For the time being we cannot take back Taiwan, so that the United States may remain for a long time in a blameworthy position, but the legality of its arbitrary occupation will certainly not be recognized.' Something very like this typically Chinese political philosophy, but arising from different moral premises, had been vainly urged on Nehru's Government by such Indian critics of his Tibetan policy as Jayprakash Narayan. For in that case the recognition of China's occupation of Tibet had been justified, at least in part, on the grounds that India was in no position to impede it.

For China the 'blameworthy position' of neighbours or rivals is an active constituent of policy, not always or necessarily to be improved upon by removing the offence. In the long view irredentism has a continuing purpose. But its actual satisfaction, or attempted satisfaction, will be measured at each point of the compass by considerations which may have little to do with territory and are all the more impervious to territorial arguments. Where the long view seems from the outside to teem with menace, the natural answer would begin with the recognition that the future, so powerfully invoked by China, is not in fact her exclusive property, and that the emergent State which is requiring from others a belated revision of attitudes is itself subject to change. There is a danger of over-simplification, however, in applying too closely that dictum of De Tocqueville concerning the permanent nature of democratic revolution, which has been encouraged by the evidence of change in Soviet Russia. Not only may the Chinese response to apparent laws of history prove radically different both in its nature and its pace. The present stage has been shown, in the precept and practice of the ruling party, to require as a condition of disciplined internal advance the maintenance of external tension, the spectre of encirclement around an incompletely established perimeter. And frontier-tensions are not always controllable, even by their engineers.

SELECT BIBLIOGRAPHY

Apart from a few classics (e.g. Cunningham on Ladakh, Drew on Kashmir, Bell on Tibet) the following short list is concerned with recent studies, a number of which themselves incorporate fuller bibliographies.

Among official publications, the essential *Report of the Officials of the Governments of India and the People's Republic of China on the Boundary Question* (Government of India, 1961) gives an idea of the formidable historical documentation which any frontier-discussion can call upon. The Indian Government's *Notes, Memoranda and Letters Exchanged Between the Governments of India and China* have appeared since September 1959 in White Papers numbering XI (to January 1965), supplemented in October 1965 by the *Notes on China's Ultimatum to India*. Available Chinese publications on the same issue include *Documents on the Sino–Indian Boundary Question* (1960) and the enlarged *Sino-Indian Boundary Question* (1962). For extracts from recent Sino–Soviet exchanges see below under Doolin, D. J. The English periodicals of the Peking Foreign Languages Press, in particular *Peking Review* and *China Reconstructs*, print Chinese views and statements.

Fruitful periodical sources are *Asian Survey, Central Asian Review, China Quarterly, Far East Quarterly, Geographical Journal, Royal Central Asian Journal* and the publications of the Royal Institute of International Affairs.

Ahmad, Z. "Tibet and Ladakh: a History," in *Far Eastern Affairs No. 3* (St. Antony's Papers No. 14). Carbondale, Ill., 1963.

Bailey, F. M. *Report on an Exploration of the North-East Frontier.* Simla, 1914.

—— *No Passport for Tibet*, London, 1957.

Bains, J. S. *India's International Disputes*. London, 1962.

Bell, Sir C. *Tibet Past and Present.* Oxford, 1924.

Bhargava, G. S. *The Battle of NEFA*. New Delhi, 1964.

Buchan, A. (*ed.*) *China and the Peace of Asia*. New York, 1965.

Chiang Kai-shek. *Soviet Russia in China.* New York, 1957.

Christian, J. L. *Modern Burma.* Berkeley, Cal., 1942.

Clyde, P. H. *The Far East.* 2nd ed., New York, 1952.

Cunningham, A. *Ladak.* London, 1854.

Dalai Lama XIV. *My Land and My People.* New York, 1962.

Dallin, D. J. *Soviet Russia and the Far East.* New York, 1948.

—— *The Rise of Russia in Asia.* New Haven, 1949.

Doolin, D. J. *Territorial Claims in the Sino-Soviet Conflict.* Stanford, 1965.

Drew, F. *The Jummoo and Kashmir Territories.* London, 1875.

Dunbar, Sir G. *Frontiers.* London, 1932.

Dutt, V. P. *China and the World.* New York, 1966.

Elwin, V. *A Philosophy for NEFA.* Shillong, 1959.

—— *India's North-East Frontier in the Nineteenth Century.* Bombay, 1959.

Fisher, M. W., Rose, L. E. and Huttenback, A. *Himalayan Battleground: Sino–Indian Rivalry in Ladakh.* New York, 1963.

FitzGerald, C. P. *The Birth of Communist China.* New York, 1966.

——*The Chinese View of their Place in the World.* London, 1964.

Friters, G. M. *Outer Mongolia and its International Position.* Baltimore, 1949.

Ginsburgs, G. and Mathos, M. *Communist China and Tibet.* The Hague, 1964.

Gould, Sir B. J. *The Jewel in the Lotus.* London, 1957.

Hsü, I. C. Y. *The Ili Crisis.* Oxford, 1965.

Hudson, G. F. "The Aksai Chin," in *Far Eastern Affairs No. 3* (St. Antony's Papers No. 14). Carbondale, Ill., 1963.

International Commission of Jurists. *The Question of Tibet and the Rule of Law.* Geneva, 1959.

—— *Tibet and the Chinese People's Republic.* Geneva, 1960.

Jackson, W. A. D. *The Russo–Chinese Borderlands.* New York, 1962.

Jain, G. L. *India Meets China in Nepal.* Bombay, 1959.

Lamb, A. *Britain and Chinese Central Asia.* London, 1960.

—— *The China–India Border.* London, 1964.

Lattimore, O. *Manchuria, Cradle of Conflict.* New York, 1932.

—— *Inner Asian Frontiers of China.* Boston, 1962.

—— *Pivot of Asia.* Boston, 1950.

—— *Studies in Frontier History.* New York, 1962.

Menon, K. P. S. *Delhi–Chungking.* Oxford, 1947.

Moraes, F. *The Revolt in Tibet*. London, 1960.

Morse, H. B. *The International Relations of the Chinese Empire*. 3 vols., London, 1910–18.

Nanporia, N. J. *The Sino–Indian Dispute*. Bombay, 1963.

Panikkar, K. M. *The Founding of the Kashmir State*. London, 1953.

—— *In Two Chinas*. London, 1960.

Patterson, G. N. *Peking versus Delhi*. New York, 1964.

Purcell, V. *South and East Asia, since 1800*. Cambridge, 1965.

Rees, D. *Korea: The Limited War*. New York, 1964.

Reid, Sir R. *History of the Frontier Areas Bordering on Assam from 1883 to 1941*. Shillong, 1942.

Richardson, H. E. *Tibet and its History*. Oxford, 1960.

Sen, C. *Tibet Disappears*. Bombay, 1960.

Snow, E. *Red Star Over China*. New York, 1961.

Tuker, Sir F. *Gorkha, the Story of the Gurkhas of Nepal*. London, 1957.

Varma, S. P. *Struggle for the Himalayas*. Delhi, 1965.

Wei, H. *China and Soviet Russia*. New York, 1956.

Wheeler, G. E. *The Modern History of Soviet Central Asia*. New York, 1965.

Whiting, A. S. *Soviet Policies in China, 1917–1924*. New York, 1954.

—— *China Crosses the Yalu*. New York, 1960.

Whiting, A. S. and Sheng Shih-ts'ai. *Sinkiang: Pawn or Pivot?* East Lansing, Mich., 1958.

Woodman, D. *The Making of Burma*. New York, 1962.

INDEX

INDEX

INDEX

INDEX

INDEX